AN INTERPRETATION OF EXISTENCE

An
INTERPRETATION
of
EXISTENCE

JOSEPH OWENS

CENTER FOR THOMISTIC STUDIES
University of St. Thomas
Houston, Texas 77006

Library of Congress Cataloging in Publication Data

Owens, Joseph.
    An interpretation of existence.

    Reprint. Originally published: Milwaukee: Bruce
Pub. Co., 1968.
    Includes bibliographical references and index.
    1. Ontology.   I. Title.
BD331.093   1985   111'.1   84-23805
ISBN 0-268-01157-5 (pbk.)

Manufactured in the United States of America

Aber doch eine *Frage, die* Frage: Ist das "Sein" ein blosses Wort und seine Bedeutung ein Dunst oder das geistige Schicksal des Abendlandes?

Martin Heidegger
Einführung in die Metaphysik, p. 28
Tübingen, 1953

But still a *question, the* question: Is "being" a mere word, and its meaning a haze or the spiritual destiny of the West?

Contents

AN INTERPRETATION OF EXISTENCE

CHAPTER I

Problem of Existence

When examining doctoral candidates, a philosophy professor made a point of asking two questions. He would say abruptly to the student: "If I came suddenly through the door and said to you, 'It is green,' what information would I be giving you?" The startled candidate, if he remained cool enough to keep his mind off the "door" and the "coming in suddenly," was expected to give a conventional answer based ultimately on Aristotle's categories — he would thereby know that the thing referred to by the "it" was colored, was perceptible, was extended in space, was present in time, was a composite of substance and accident, was different from non-green things and was the subject of many other more or less obvious relations. The examiner would then follow abruptly with the second question: "If I simply said to you, 'It is,' would I be giving you any information at all?"

This second question was meant to prove much more difficult than the first. It could trigger a reply along the general lines of the well-known development given it in Parmenides' poem, in which an impressive array of predicates was, in recent if not too exact parlance, "unpacked" from the simple assertion ἔστιν — "it is." On the other hand, the question could be met against the background of Kant's frequently quoted claim that being "is not a concept of something which could be added to the concept of a thing."[1] In the latter context the answer might be drawn out according to the pattern of the discussions that followed upon the widely read symposium papers of W. Kneale and G. E. Moore on existence as a predicate.[2] In an extreme view that has obtained prominence in this setting, existence is neither a real nor a logical predicate. How, then, could it give any new or genuine information about a thing? How could even human existence become, in the modern existentialist trends, the most important of all considerations, predominating over everything based upon essential characteristics?

But apart from remote and recent historical backgrounds, does not the mere assertion "it is" sound linguistically awkward in English? Would not a little reflection be required for the average person to realize what one is trying to say? Nevertheless, a student majoring in philosophy, acquainted as he should be with modern debates on the concept of existence, would not be in any doubt about what the mini-sentence was attempting to assert. To express the notion in idiomatic English, he has only to change over to the verb "exists." Linguistically the verbal form "is" requires completion in English by a further predicate word, as in the expression "It is green" or "It is warm."

In Latin or Greek, on the other hand, the third person of the corresponding verb may be readily used without further

---

[1] *Critique of Pure Reason*, B 626; tr. Norman Kemp Smith. The mini-sentence may be seen used, with the "is" italicized, in Hazel E. Barnes' translation of Jean-Paul Sartre, *Being and Nothingness* (New York, 1956), pp. li (xlix) and lxviii (lxvi); cf. p. 84. It may be seen also in Sydney Hook, *The Quest for Being* (New York, 1961), p. 154.

[2] "Is Existence a Predicate?" *Proceedings of the Aristotelian Society*, Supplement, XV (1936), pp. 154–188.

predicative determination, as in the expression "*Deus est*," or in Parmenides' use of ἔστιν. In translating the notion idiomatically into English, however, "exists" has to be used instead of "is" — "God exists" and "It exists," respectively. If the setting permits the use of "there" before the verb "is," no problem of course arises. "In the Middle East there is tension" and "In the Middle East tension exists," are equivalent in meaning.[3] But in the present case no possibility of inserting a "there" is offered. "There it is" or "There is it" will not do. The idiomatic expression for the notion is "It exists."

So rephrased, the statement is in fact idiomatic. But again, is it really meaningful? Here crucial difficulty is encountered. If one may be conceded fully for the moment[4] that "It exists" expresses idiomatically what "It is" tries awkwardly to state, one still has to face the real problem, a problem that soon surfaces in the midst of choppy waters. It is the problem of what content there is in the notion of existence. A case readily can be made, and has been made repeatedly in the

---

[3] Cf.: ". . . among the forms by the use of which one most clearly and explicitly asserts the existence of objects of a certain sort . . . are the forms 'There is an N,' 'Something is an N,' . . ." W. Sellars, "Grammar and Existence: A Preface to Ontology," *Mind*, LIX (1960), 508. Similarly "'A exists,' for example, will be equivalent to 'A has existence.'" Bertrand Russell, "On the Relations of Universals to Particulars," *Proceedings of the Aristotelian Society*, XII (1912), 5. As G. E. Moore (*art. cit.*, p. 176), notes, "existence" as a predicate in the logical sense is equivalent to what is meant by "the word 'exists,' and other finite parts of the verb 'to exist.'"

[4] A difference between "being" and "existence" was maintained in the controversies originating with Giles of Rome and Henry of Ghent in the last quarter of the thirteenth century, as may be seen in the formulation of their problem in the terms *esse essentiae* and *esse existentiae*. The earlier Russell, *The Principles of Mathematics* (2nd ed. London, 1937), pp. 449–450, maintained a similar distinction. Meinong's "principle of the independence of *Sosein* from *Sein*" in "The Theory of Objects," translated in R. Chisholm's *Realism and the Background of Phenomenology* (Glencoe, Ill.: The Free Press, 1960), p. 82, parallels Giles' stand (*Quodl.*, V, 3, Louvain, 1646, p. 273a) that a nature has of itself sufficient actuality to be understood but not enough to exist in reality. For the case that on the contrary all being is completely identified with existence, see my study of the problem in *An Elementary Christian Metaphysics* (Milwaukee: The Bruce Publishing Company, 1963), pp. 40–140.

past, to show that the concept of existence is entirely empty.[5] In Kant's (*ibid.*, B 627) much discussed example, one hundred existent thalers have no more conceptual content than one hundred possible ones. Existence, this reasoning insists, *adds* nothing to the thing. It merely places the thing in itself.

Yet is not the placing of a thing in itself something quite meaningful? Are you not giving pertinent information when in this sense you say, without further qualification, that a thing exists? Is not that statement meaningfully different from the assertion that the thing does not exist? Can you not at once discern a sharp contrast from this standpoint between the statements "Whooping cranes still exist" and "Passenger pigeons do not any longer exist"? Is the difference not meaningful? Would there not be a radical change in *meaning* if the negatives were reversed and the sentences read "Whooping cranes no longer exist," while "Passenger pigeons still exist"?

Certainly, then, there is a definite meaning, easily recognizable, in the assertion that something exists. Often that is what one directly wants to know in an inquiry.[6] One may wish to know first whether flying saucers exist, and only afterwards be prompted to investigate what they are. With the Loch Ness monster, the initial inquiry is whether it actually does exist. Only after acquiring positive information in that regard would one seriously undertake to investigate what type of animal it is. On the other hand, knowing perfectly well who Socrates, son of Phaenarete and husband of Xanthippe, pur-

---

[5] "The reason that Existence must be empty, diaphanous, blank, and, in sum, *nil*, resides in its definitory contrast with Essence. . . . There is no nature left for Existence, . . ." Donald C. Williams, "Dispensing with Existence," *The Journal of Philosophy*, LIX (1962), 753. Cf.: "If we stop with existence, and refuse to go any further, the existent is a perfect and absolute blank, and to say that only this exists is equivalent to saying that nothing exists." J. M. E. McTaggart, *The Nature of Existence* (Cambridge, England: Cambridge University Press, 1921), I, p. 60.

[6] E.g.: "You can imagine all sorts of cases where what is wanted is to know whether or not some thing does exist . . . not whether it has a long or short snout, but whether or not it is extinct or extant." M. Kiteley, "Is Existence a Predicate?" *Mind*, LXXIII (1964), p. 365.

ported to be, the historian of Greek philosophy may well ask, in the wake of Dupréel's book *La Légende Socratique*,[7] whether or not Socrates really existed. Sometimes in the case of conjectured links in organic evolution, the important question is whether in fact they did exist or not. Correspondingly, the observed existence of the previously conjectured planet Neptune, and the nonexistence of the conjectured intramercurial planet Vulcan, have been readily distinguishable answers to astronomical questions which actually have been raised.

There should be no doubt, therefore, that the existence or nonexistence of a thing has a pertinent meaning all of its own. Yet the difficulties raised in the many and persistent controversies about content in the concept of existence give pause for abundant reflection. They cannot be brushed aside as irrelevant. Have they not at least an acute relevance in showing beyond cavil that the concept of existence cannot be assessed like other concepts? Knowing whether or not a lungfish exists does not add anything further to one's conception of what a lungfish is. Existence does not in fact, as Kant has so clearly shown, add any new conceptual knowledge to what is already known. This content of one hundred dollars remains exactly the same — one hundred times one hundred cents — whether the dollars really exist in your pocket or are just imagined in a pipe dream. The real existence of the dollars, even though this may be the most important factor involved, obviously adds no conceptual content to their meaning.

Difficulties in logical notation, moreover, arise when one tries to formalize existence as a predicate. One may claim on metaphysical grounds that existence unquestionably has to be regarded as a perfection, with the consequent requirement of a special predicate letter, say Q, to represent it. But how could one then quantify existentially the propositional function Qx?

---

[7] Eugène Dupréel, *La Légende Socratique et les Sources de Platon,* (Brussels, 1922).

Unless one is willing to admit that the quantifier has nothing to do with the existence predicated, one would at best be introducing a bit of redundancy. $(\exists x)Qx$ would mean there exists an x that is existing, just as $(\exists x)Bx$ would mean there exists an x that is brown. If the quantifier symbolizes what is expressed in ordinary language by "there is," the grammatical predicate "exists," when phrased in what has just been seen to be its equivalent "there is," at once is shown in the symbolism to be an intolerable and useless repetition. One is merely saying "There is, there is, an x." No addition in meaning is made manifest. Unless special circumstances demanded rhetorical emphasis on the "there is" by repetition ("there is — I repeat, there is") the redundant phrasing would not be used in ordinary language. Accordingly, a logician, eliminating existence as a predicative perfection, is able to maintain: "The word 'existence' is not a symbol for anything which can be either a constituent or a component of a simple proposition. It is only a logical auxiliary symbol."[8]

How, then, can the concept of existence be meaningful? How can the assertion "It exists" give you any information at all? In what way does existence confront the human intellect's gaze? Is it a stubborn fact resistant to human intellection yet without meaning for it? Or is it entirely diaphanous and translucent, indeed there, and undoubtedly necessary to allow an object to come under intellectual vision, but in itself not something upon which the intellect could ponder? May not one readily admit existence as a fact, and still main-

---

[8] W. Kneale, art. cit., p. 164. Cf.: "Any primitive predication of existence is necessarily redundant if the normal meanings of our other logical concepts are accepted." Jaakko Hintikka, "Studies in the Logic of Existence and Necessity," The Monist, L (1966), 66. On the other hand, the case that existential quantification is coextensive with existence is by no means airtight; cf. ". . . there is no general correspondence between existentially quantified formulae and existence statements." Sellars, art. cit., p. 507. ". . . not even all (so-called) existential quantification over singular term variables has the force of an existence statement." Ibid. Reprinted in Sellars' Science, Perception and Reality (London & New York, 1963), p. 255. Nor can there be different degrees of existence, if it is only a uniformly applicable symbol.

tain that it is utterly useless in philosophical investigation and, accordingly, should be banned from the realm of philosophical discourse?[9]

Granted, consequently, that one knows clearly the fact that some things such as whooping cranes exist, and that in the same context one knows just as clearly that others like passenger pigeons or dodos do not exist, and granted that as a rule one can clearly distinguish between the two situations, is not an intriguing problem faced when one becomes immersed in the interpretation of the fact? What kind of knowledge can the fact hope to provide if it manifests no new conceptual content? How is it at all to result in philosophical gain, if it offers nothing on which the intellect's conceptualizing activity can concentrate? How can it do anything else than tantalize the appetite with an illusory promise of perhaps the most exotic of intellectual food, yet in a menu that does not fall within the modest means of an authentically philosophical budget? Will not what it actually serves, on the contrary, appear rather as an utterly tasteless and indigestible characteristic in things, containing nothing upon which intellectual teeth in their ordinarily recognized activity can chew?

What worthwhile results can existence lead to, philosophically, if from the standpoint of conceptualization it is re-

---

[9] Hence the appeal to "banish the term 'Being' from the vocabulary of philosophy." Sidney Hook, "The Quest for 'Being,'" *Proceedings of the XIth International Congress of Philosophy* (Amsterdam & Louvain, 1953), XIV, 18. The paper is reprinted in Hook's *The Quest for Being* (New York, 1961), p. 147. For a still more extreme assessing of the situation, cf.: "Existence is irrational for a deeper and more intrinsic reason than because one part of it may not be deducible from another: any part, and all its parts together, are irrational in merely existing, and in being otherwise than as essences are, that is, identical with themselves and endowed with that formal being which it is impossible that anything, whatever it may be, should not possess." George Santayana, *The Realm of Essence* (New York, 1927), p. 21. "Existence itself is a surd, external to the essence which it may illustrate and irrelevant to it; . . ." *Ibid.*, pp. 109–110. On the skepticism involved in this view, see Armand Maurer, *Recent Philosophy*, ed. E. Gilson (New York: Random House, 1966), pp. 617–618. The sharp contrast between existence and "formal being" should be noted.

garded merely as an observable fact without definable meaning, a surd that eludes further intellectual penetration? How can any consequences be "unpacked" when the hope chest, though macroscopically visible in its gross bulk, remains locked to a genuinely conceptual representation of its contents? Yet existence, as has been seen, has a sharply distinguishable meaning from nonexistence, even though the meaning does not appear in the conceptualization of the thing.

Clearly, then, the interpretation of existence has its problems. Prima facie, they are intriguing enough. But are they not more than just intriguing? Have they not poignant relevance to the basic problems of human destiny, especially in today's context? The existence of things is admittedly known. It is a fact. Does not the fact in the present philosophical setting raise two marked alternatives? In the one alternative, will not the information given by existence be restricted to the bare and philosophically trivial contingency that something happens to be there, in the guise of a mere historical event? But in the other alternative, will not existence be pregnant with the most far-reaching and all-important of philosophical consequences? Will it not purport to be the one key to knowledge of what matters most in philosophy? Will it not claim to be identical with freedom, with subjectivity, with God?

Both alternatives have flourished in the course of Western philosophical enterprise. Both have been vigorously, at times acrimoniously, defended. Their implications, moreover, have been tellingly confronted in the blunt conclusion that "the only viable alternative to dispensing with Existence is to decide that it is God."[10] Does not this mean either that existence is to be ruled out of philosophical consideration altogether, or else that it is to be thoroughly identified with the divine nature? If allowed in this way a meaning of its own,

---

[10] Donald C. Williams, art. cit., p. 754.

will it not require, philosophically, the rational and fully demonstrable conclusion that God exists? Surely against this background its interpretation is much more than just an interesting philosophical problem. Is there not a chance that somehow, in Heidegger's words, it may on its own level hold the spiritual destiny of the West?

Does not this clear voicing of the alternatives, then, ring with the challenge of a bugle call? Does it not present vividly issues that are actual, urging one on to appropriate metaphysical investigation of their ramifications? Is the humble fact of the existence of chairs and tables, trees and stones, mice and men, something that may be merely noted as an unimportant aside and then entirely disregarded for purposes of scientific and philosophical inquiry? Is their existence like the wheels that have been so necessary for a plane to get off the ground, but which disappear once the craft is airborne, in order not to offer any impediment to smooth flight? Does existence reappear only when the landing gear is necessary to bring the physicist or the logician back to the level on which he dines and chats, and plays bridge just as Hume played backgammon? Or, on the contrary, does the lowly existence of everyday things offer on the philosophical level "the sole direct path leading our minds to the throne of God?"[11]

Furthermore, if the existence so readily known in the things that come under one's daily scrutiny provides the one purely intellectual path of man to God; may it not thereby hold many more consequences of similar importance in regard to problems concerning human destiny and the human soul, and the more intricate aspects of questions about the currently discussed role of historicity and freedom and subjectivity? Are not these issues crucial in the present Christian context?

In the current ecumenical mentality, are not dozens of Christian traditions and groupings aiming at unity in the

---

[11] Louis-Marie Régis, *Epistemology* (New York: Macmillan, 1959), p. 300.

midst of deep-seated religious disagreement on doctrines that are all attributed to the workings of the Holy Spirit yet are often in sharp contradiction to one another (e.g., the pope is infallible, the pope is not infaliible; there is transubstantiation in the Eucharist, there is no transubstantiation in the Eucharist)? Under this welter of divergence in the rule of religious faith, does not one welcome a cool, rational assurance that God exists and is knowable in his attributes and ever present activity, and a similar assurance that the existence of one's soul is perpetual?

If such knowledge is obtainable in a public and communicable way, if it is established by cogent and unaided demonstration and is therefore immune to disturbance by even the most obviously sincere reports of reciprocally contradictory religious inspirations, is it not a type of knowledge devoutly to be wished? Is not purely philosophical knowledge in these supremely important areas, knowledge wholly unaffected on its own level by differing religious and theological views, knowledge rationally controllable and not subject to becoming outdated, a great desideratum in the present situation? Is it not currently imperative?

No matter how strong and precise one's own religious faith may be, that of other persons does in fact make diametrically opposite claims, all on the rationally unassailable ground of the working of the Holy Spirit. But there are no instant metaphysicians. The principles of metaphysical reasoning are open to public inspection. Their development is slow, laborious, and cogent. The years of training and absorption required for their way of thinking engenders a mentality both sure of itself and flexible enough to remain the same in direction throughout all the changing circumstances of time, just as the wisdom of Heraclitus remained one and the same in penetrating the ever changing cosmos through a perpetual seesaw of opposites. If an interpretation of existence promises this kind of knowledge, is not the topic amply worth investigating? Surely the question how the everyday existence of things around us is to be interpreted deserves thoughtful and philosophically sympathetic consideration.

Some of the above considerations, it is true, look out on areas that not so long ago lay by more or less tacit agreement outside the purview of purely philosophical interest. Yet today, when so much attention in philosophy is being directed toward problems traditionally regarded as religious, and when institutes for the study of religious experience are mushrooming across the land, can the facets that open upon these topics be ignored in a comprehensively philosophical investigation of existence? Would not closing one's eyes to them be the sign of an anemic inability to take full part in the life of one's day and age?

There is no question, one need hardly remark, of substituting metaphysical knowledge in any way for faith, or of attempting to have philosophy do the work of religion. In this respect metaphysics can minister at best only to the solid bone structure. For a Christian, the life is breathed into the structure from elsewhere. The flesh is of other origin. But although the life of the skeletal frame is sublimated into the life of the whole organism, its own norms of health remain intact. Just as in every other instance, grace, while building upon nature and working through nature, does not at all destroy the functioning of the natural order.

Metaphysical knowledge about God and the soul retains its own unshakable certainty when it is pursued in a life lived through faith. It can provide for the health of the skeletal structure in the noospherical conditions of present-day cultural activity, just as technological achievements provide for the welfare of the human organism in the hazardous surroundings of space travel. In the great divergence of religiously inspired views around him, then, may not the metaphysician have full confidence in his science on its own level, just as the physicist and the chemist have in theirs?

The interpretation of the everyday fact that things exist is in view of all this a problem that has to be faced coolly and penetratingly. The existence most obvious to human cognition and mostly widely conceded in today's philosophical orbit is of course the existence of sensibly perceptible objects.[12] These are things that can be seen and heard and touched, such as mats and cats, and mice and men. That they exist is obvious when one is perceiving them. But though the fact is evident, the interpretation of the fact has ranged to opposite extremes of the philosophical spectrum. If on the one hand existence is allowed but the syncategorematic role of an auxiliary logical symbol, how can there be any more question of higher degrees of existence than of degrees of "and" or of "or"? Would not one be left with only the commonplace and often unpalatable or unsightly existence that one encounters in lowly sensible things?

In this perspective what else could be done except to acknowledge existence as a brute fact and as a framework for the thing's intelligible features, and straightway disregard it as philosophically trivial? Would one then have the least hesitation in shying away grimly and of set purpose from the intricate debates that have flooded philosophical literature from the time of Parmenides, and in pleading with the metaphysician not to push the topic onward to any alleged higher levels of being, but rather to "leave us in our humble and tarnished frame of existence"?[13] But if, on the other hand, the existence that seems so common and workaday should turn out to be the object of intellectual consideration that

---

[12] Further discussion of this assertion may be found in my paper, "The Range of Existence," *Proceedings of the Seventh Inter-American Congress of Philosophy* (Quebec, 1967), pp. 44–45; 53–54, nn. 10–15.

[13] T. S. Eliot, *Murder in the Cathedral*, 2nd ed. (London, 1936), p. 20.

is "the richest and has the most spectacular destiny,"[14] if as in Heidegger's claim it should be the most important of all themes for the destiny of Western culture, would not one be missing what is best in the philosophical enterprise if one neglected it? Both alternatives have presented strong prima facie cases, and appear as extremes in the intellectual spectrum. Does the truth then lie in either extreme, or somewhere in the area between them, or is it spread in various ways throughout the multiple different vibrations of the light waves? At least the fact of existence raises its questions, and the interpretation of the fact is basic as a metaphysical problem.

---

[14] Régis, op. cit.

CHAPTER II

Grasp of Existence

From the considerations in the preceding chapter, one may already suspect that a grasp of the existence of things does not originate in any concept. Conceptually, as has been noted, one hundred dollars are the same whether the dollars really exist or not; neither does the concept of a house become different when the house comes into existence.[1] Offering no content that can be apparent in the conceptualization of a thing, how could existence ever make its entry into the mind through a concept? How could it become known in the way in which a thing's nature and size and qualities and other categorical perfections are grasped? Yet know it we do. In what manner, then, is its impact made upon our minds?

On the level of sensation we undoubtedly see, hear, touch, smell, and taste existent things. They are perceived in no other way than as existent. A nonexistent thing could not be perceived through these senses. But in sensation existence

---

[1] See Chapter I, nn. 1, 5, and 8. Cf.: "It makes sense and is true to say that my future house will be a better one if it is insulated than if it is not insulated; but what could it mean to say that it will be a better house if it exists than if it does not?" Norman Malcolm, "Anselm's Ontological Arguments," *The Philosophical Review*, LXIX (1960), p. 43.

is not known separately or distinctly. Rather, the existent thing is perceived globally, holistically. Our intellect, on the other hand, can consider the thing and the existence separately. It can contrast the one with the other and ask questions about their relation to each other. In fact, lengthy and animated discussions on problems of essence versus existence stretch back through the past seven centuries of metaphysics.

Unlike the senses, then, the intellect surely must have some way of grasping the existence of a thing in meaningful distinction from the thing itself. If it did not, what basis would it have for contrasting the one with the other? Although knowledge of existence, like all other human knowledge, originates in sensation, the intellectual penetration of the data in distinguishing between the thing itself and its existence seems to indicate clearly enough a distinct way of grasping the existential dimension. If this way is not conceptualization — and the case against its being this is here compelling — what kind of intellectual activity can it be?

Perhaps an approach after the fashion of linguistic analysis may be the easiest and most profitable. At least language is public and readily open to scrutiny. In language, aspects of a thing that are originally known through concepts are expressed by single words. Color, size, substance, proximity, place, time, all convey clearly etched notions of the thing. But can any isolated word in English carry the type of meaning involved in our mini-sentence "It is," or "It exists"? Here you are faced not with a mere combination of two concepts, the concept of "something" as represented by the "it," on the one hand, and the concept of "being" or "existence" on the other — no, adding "it" and "existence" to each other does not tell you the "it" exists. The two may add up to the compound concept of "existing thing," but even then the combination does not tell you that the existent thing actually exists. Paradoxically, "existence" as a noun or "existent" as an adjective does not seem able to carry the message one might expect from analogy with other concepts. The difficulties in the efforts to make the ontological argument prove the existence of God bear eloquent witness to this anomaly. No matter how perfectly one may conceive existence, even on the level of infinite perfection, one has good ground for hesitating to concede that one has thereby shown that anything exists. Words like "brown" and "cow" regularly convey the notions they were coined to express. But "existence" and "existent" do not always, it would seem, succeed in accomplishing a corresponding task.

May not one think of and talk of a mountain of gold really existent in the Himalayas, for example, without knowing that it does exist there, and even when convinced that it does not exist there? May not one envisage a really existent country home, not just an imaginary one, although it has not yet been built? May not one legitimately form a notion of really existent dodos, and then deny existence to them? "There are no existent dodos" seems to make good enough sense. Yet problems arise. "But there are no dodos" would seem to convey exactly the same sense as "but there are no existent dodos," rendering the adjective "existent" superfluous in the manner noted in the preceding chapter. The expression "existent dodos" may serve to distinguish them from "imaginary dodos" as an object of discussion, but it does not seem to establish their existence until a sentence is used to say that they do exist.

In a word, the compound concept "existent thing" is not in itself sufficient to cope satisfactorily with the thing's existence. Only when asserted through a sentence is the full force of what is meant by "existence" seen in the thing. When that is done, the adjective becomes superfluous. "Existent things exist" carries no more meaning than "Things exist." Yet unless the phrase "existent things" is spotlighting what has been grasped already through the knowledge expressed in the sentence asserting that these things do exist, the notion fails to click. It leaves a question mark about what it is meant to express. To speak of "existing whooping cranes" in a way that conveys the full import of what is meant by their existence, one has to be resuming in the adjective "existent" one's already established knowledge expressed in the sentence that they do exist. Detached from the knowledge that they in fact exist, the "existence" of whooping cranes would carry no more authentically existential meaning than the "existence" of dodos or dinosaurs. When expressed by a single word, the notion of existence seems unable to do the work expected of it, unless it is calling attention to a fact that is expressed in sentence form.

What is originally meant by existence, these considerations indicate, can be communicated only through a sentence. Cats exist, mice exist, men exist. The verbal form required is one that shows that a predicate is being asserted of a subject. Any other combination of words is insufficient, for, as has just been seen, assertion is more than a mere addition of concepts. The sum total of what is expressed by the concepts alone, e.g. "cats" and "existence," leaves a crucial remainder. Not just cats plus existence, but the fact that cats exist, is stated. Something over and above the conceptual content is expressed by the sentence form. A fact, accordingly, is something more than the sum total of what is expressed in the concepts it involves.[2]

A sentence, then, expresses something more than what is expressed by all its words taken separately. What is the mental construct that it represents? The construct is called a

---

[2] Cf.: "The only other sort of object you come across in the world is what we call *facts*, and facts are the sort of things that are asserted or denied by propositions, and are not properly entities at all in the same sense in which their constituents are . . . the knowing of facts is a different sort of thing from the knowing of simples." Bertrand Russell, "The Philosophy of Logical Atomism," *The Monist*, XXIV (1919), pp. 365–366.

proposition. As a unitary proposition it is contrasted with its terms, the subject and predicate, and with the copula that joins the terms. All these elements are distinct notions and are expressed in the sentence by different words. But the construct taken as a whole has, from the viewpoint of the logician, a value that its elements, taken either singly or in sum total, do not have. This is the value of truth or falsity. The value attaches only to propositions, not to terms.

How is the appropriate value known? The proposition is held before the mind's reflexive gaze and compared with what is seen in the actual world. If from the viewpoint of the copula it is in agreement with what is found there, it is known to be true. If it is in disagreement, it is understood to be false. The weatherman may announce on the newscast, "Sunny weather prevails all over the area." Looking out the window you see the pouring rain, and you qualify the proposition as false. You explain to yourself that the report was issued at the weather observatory several hours before. It is the actual existence of rainy weather, as you perceive it here and now, that makes you reject the proposition. The proposition is worded to express the weather conditions as they actually exist, but does not do so. You have the means of perceiving and of grasping intellectually that it is raining outside. This knowledge you formulate in a proposition contrary to the television announcement. You say to yourself "It is raining." You can take a second look at the actual weather to be sure, compare your proposition with what you see, and in consequence accept your own proposition as true.

The proposition, as has been already noted, is a construct of the human mind. Unlike a concept, it is necessarily a complex structure. But it is complex in a different way from the mere combination of concepts in a "frisky cat" or a "purple pine." It is different either through asserting the one concept's content of the other's, or through simply asserting the existence of what is represented by a concept. An example of the first would be "The cat is frisky," and an instance of the second, "Whooping cranes exist." In the latter case the proposition asserts existence of its subject. But propositions of both kinds are accepted as true or rejected as false on the basis of what one knows through looking at the actual situation, through observing or concluding to what is there in the actual world. Does one not thereby tacitly acknowledge possession of the means to know that the thing actually exists, or actually has the predicated nature or activity?

What is expressed in a proposition, then, is a type of knowledge that the intellect is able to attain about its objects, a type of knowledge that cannot be expressed in a concept or communicated in English by a single word. It is a type of knowledge that can be mentally expressed only in the synthesis of a proposition and communicated verbally in a sentence. A fact, accordingly, is synthetic in character. To be grasped by the mind it will presumably require a type of intellectual activity that is correspondingly synthetic in its very nature as a cognitive function.

What is this special way of knowing, this presumably synthetic intellectual activity? It is obviously the knowledge that something exists, or is endowed with the predicate in question, in the case of positive knowledge. If for the moment the problem of negative knowledge may be left aside, and the consideration of predicates other than existence be postponed till later, one may begin by concentrating on the knowledge that something exists. How is this knowledge to be designated? Of course it may be called the knowledge of existence, or the intuition of existence. But is there no single word available to designate one's knowledge that something exists?

Oddly perhaps at first sight, there seems to be no single ordinary language word to express the notion. This in itself suggests, significantly, a peculiar status for one's original in-

tellectual grasp of existence. Terms express concepts, and here
one is concerned with an activity that is specified by an object
eluding expression by a simple concept. The object, namely
that something exists, may be referred to as the existence of
the thing in question, but with the reservations already considered. Mention of "the existence of the thing" does not
tell you that the thing exists unless it is focusing attention on
what is grasped through the synthetic type of knowledge communicated by a sentence. Similarly, this object may be referred to by the single word "fact," but with similar reservations. Etymologically "fact" means something that has been
done or made. The noun refers to something that requires
assertion by a verbal form. Unless it is taking up again what
was known in the assertion, it is not expressing any genuine
factual status. One would still have to show that the fact
mentioned actually is a fact.

However, the ways in which the object of the intellect's
synthetic activity can be referred to in ordinary language by
single words like "existence" or "fact" suggest that a single
term also may be found for the activity itself, at least to serve
the purposes of philosophical reflection. In philosophical
treatment a single term is imperative for smooth discussion.
Is there any one word available in technical philosophic
vocabulary to express the notion of "knowledge that something exists"? There is one available from the writings of
Aquinas. It is the term "judgment."[3] Originally the word

---

[3] "To know this relationship of conformity is to judge that a thing is such
or is not, which is to compose and divide; therefore the intellect does not
know truth except by composing and dividing through its judgment. If the
judgment is in accordance with things it will be true, . . ." St. Thomas,
In I Perihermeneias, lect. 3, Leonine no. 9; tr. Jean T. Oesterle, p. 33. "Now
names of this kind signify something, namely, certain simple concepts (although
the things they signify are composite), and therefore are not true or false
unless 'to be' or 'not to be' is added, by which a judgment of the intellect
is expressed." Ibid., no. 13, p. 34. Cf.: "C'est . . . dans un jugement
d'existence, que l'intuition de l'être se produit" ("It is . . . in a judgment
of existence that the intuition of being occurs"). J. Maritain, Le Paysan de
la Garonne (Paris: Gabalda, 1966), p. 205.

meant something else, a courtroom decision. In ordinary language its regular use is concerned with estimating alternatives or deciding among them. But in a technical use the term is appropriated to denote the intellectual activity by which the existence of things is originally known. Just as the substance of a thing and the color of a thing and its relations and other categorical traits are grasped by the intellect through conceptualization, so the thing's existence is indeed grasped intellectually, but not through conceptualization, at least originally. The apprehension of existence requires a different kind of intellectual activity. To designate this activity, whatever it may turn out to be, may we be permitted for convenience to use the Thomistic term "judgment"? Unsatisfactory though the word may be, and awkward in its application, it has not as yet been replaced by any even remotely suitable substitute.

There is, however, a further complication. Even in this technical sphere the term "judgment" has two different though closely related meanings. Unless these meanings are kept carefully distinguished, they will cause intolerable confusion. Alongside the sense of "the knowledge that something exists," the term "judgment" can readily have a meaning that coincides with a "proposition" in the use discussed above. You can compare your judgment that the weather is cold with the actual thermometer reading, and conclude that the judgment was wrong. You attribute your mistake to have remained too long in a warm room. Accordingly, you are comparing a mental construct, made on the basis of your own

---

Aquinas also uses the phrase "second operation" of the intellect to designate this mental act. See In I Sententiarum, d. 38, q. 1, a. 3, Solut. (ed. Mandonnet, I, 903); In Boethii de Trinitate, V. 3 (ed. Decker, p. 182.9–10). For a judgment in the sense of a proposition, he regularly uses "enunciation," as may be seen throughout the commentary on Perihermeneias and in the commentary on the Sentences. A discussion of recent objections against the "Hume-Brentano-Gilson thesis," as the doctrine just seen in Aquinas on judgment is labeled by Geach in "Assertion," The Philosophical Review, LXXIV (1965), p. 459, may be found in my paper "The Range of Existence," Proceedings of the Seventh Inter-American Congress of Philosophy (Quebec, 1967), I, p. 55.

sensory reactions, with the actual existence of weather conditions to which you have concluded from the reading of
a trustworthy scientific instrument. The correct judgment of
a few moments earlier would have been, "It feels cold to
me." That judgment would have corresponded exactly with
what you knew as you confronted the actual situation. The
judgment would have agreed with what was grasped through
the intellectual activity called "judgment" in the preceding
paragraph.

So, when you look out and see that it is raining, you can
compare the ensuing mental construct with what you are
actually seeing, and say that your judgment is true. In this
sense a "judgment" obviously means what in logic is technically called a proposition. In the sense in which the term
was used for the mental activity, on the other hand, "judgment" means the actual knowing that the weather is rainy.
The two senses of the term are intimately related, for judgment, in the sense of a proposition, is meant to picture statically the dynamic and temporally conditioned grasp of existence, existence that is always progressing from the past
through the present into the future. While the term "proposition" can have only the static sense of a mental construct,
then, the term "judgment" can be used in both significations.

This particular difference in the use of the two terms is of
telling importance. The logical term "proposition" misses
entirely the other and metaphysically important sense of the
term "judgment." You can take the proposition "It is raining," call it a judgment, and analyze it into its elements, even
while you are looking out into the bright sunshine of a cloud-
less summer afternoon. The proposition by no means obliges
you to judge that it is raining. Accordingly, "judgment," in
its technical sense of knowing existence, is a different activity
from the constructing of propositions. This allows a proposition to be formed as a static picture of what you judge in

things. The static proposition, or judgment in this sense, may
then be compared closely with what is known through your
original and dynamic judgment, that is, with the judgment
in the sense of an intellectual activity by which existence is
originally known. In this way one may see whether the construct is true or false, that is, whether it agrees or disagrees
with what is grasped through the mental activity of judgment.

As the above examples make clear, the time element enters
significantly into the object of judgment, when judgment is
understood in the sense of the intellectual activity through
which existence is originally known. A logician may prefer a
tenseless world,[4] but a metaphysician has to take existence as
it is offered to his scrutiny in the real as well as the cognitional universe. So regarded, real existence is in fact continually passing through the present into the future. The
proposition "It is raining" may be true today and false tomorrow, in accordance with the successive existence of ever
changing weather conditions. It is the existence of things here
and now that is originally grasped through the intellectual
activity designated by the term "judgment" in this metaphysically basic and important sense. Born of the past and pregnant
with the future, the existence immediately known in sensible

---

[4] See Quine, "Designation and Existence," *The Journal of Philosophy*,
XXXVI (1939), p. 701. Cf.: "The most decisive consideration is that we are
able to form classes of things that are not contemporary with one another."
Quine, in *Proceedings of the Seventh Inter-American Congress of Philosophy*,
I, p. 62. But the fact that Rommel, Napoleon, Caesar, and Hannibal may be
included in the class of great generals surely need not mean anything more,
from the viewpoint of existence, than that these generals may be thought of
at the present moment and encompassed by the one generic concept. That is
sufficient for the purposes of logic. The objects have contemporary existence
in the mind that is thinking about them. There seems no reason why contemporary real existence also should be required. Cf.: "But if something is a
fact, it is a fact, even if the verb in the that-clause is in the past or future
tense." Wilfrid Sellars, "Time and the World Order," *Minnesota Studies in
the Philosophy of Science*, III (1962), p. 528. Present real existence, accordingly,
is not meant: " 'Exist' here is intended in a *tenseless* sense, *i.e.*, in the sense
in which it would be true that there exist red surfaces even if *at present*
none exist, provided that some red surfaces existed in the past." Arthur Pap,
"Indubitable Existential Statements," *Mind*, LV (1946), p. 236, n. 1.

things presents itself as a continuous and unidirectional flux.

The lines are now taking shape for a consistent picture of human intellectual activity as it grasps the things that confront it. *What* things are is known through conceptualization. *That* they exist is known through a different activity technically called judgment. What is known *dynamically* through judgment is represented *statically* in a proposition. This allows the proposition to be compared with what is actually being judged, in order to determine whether the proposition is true or false. Accordingly the activity of judgment, originally at least, is an act of apprehension, of knowing, of intuiting. The objection, "What criterion have you for knowing that your judgment is true?" when applied to the intellectual activity, misses this point. It confuses the two senses of "judgment," equating judgment merely with a proposition.

Rather, the existence of the thing, as known through judgment in the metaphysically basic sense of the term, is itself the criterion for evaluating the proposition. The objection presupposes that you have to know existence in some other way, presumably through conceptualization, and then compare the results with your judgment. But the way in which existence is originally known is precisely what is meant by judgment in this metaphysically important sense. To the judgment so understood, no object that could be described as an "existential hyaline"[5] is offered. On the contrary, the existence is clearly knowable in its own right. The razor-edge precision of the difference between to be and not to be makes it sharply discernible, from the viewpoint of judgment. It is knowable and discernible in the way the present actuality of the whooping crane is understood in contrast to the nonexistence of the

---

[5] For this viewpoint, see Donald C. Williams, "Dispensing with Existence," *The Journal of Philosophy*, LIX (1962), p. 754. Its claim is that existence in order to be contemplated has to be "fattened" or "loaded" with meaning from the realm of essence, "somewhat as a microscopist must stain the transparent tissues to make them visible." *Ibid.*

passenger pigeon. From this viewpoint no tincture of characteristics from the thing's essence is required to make the
existence observable. In fact, none is even able to make the
slightest contribution in this respect. Only from the viewpoint
of conceptual knowledge may existence be assessed as a hyaline.
Diaphanous to authentically conceptual apprehension, it can
be represented conceptually only in the colors of other objects, such as actuality, or perfection, or in the most general
fashion of all as "something." For judgment, though, it has
decidedly original meaning. In a word, judgment as the apprehension of existence is not a rubber-stamp endorsement of
something already known through conceptualization. It is
itself the original apprehension of existence.

Nevertheless, the two intellectual activities, conceptualization and judgment, always accompany each other. A nature in
abstraction from existence is just not there to be grasped, and
existence apart from something it actuates is nowhere found
in the range of human experience. Both appear and are
grasped as different aspects of the one existent thing. The
question whether the distinction between them is real or not
does not arise at the present moment. The immediate point
is that they are aspects known through two different kinds
of intellectual activity, one of which is communicated through
simple terms, the other through sentences.

What bearing does the distinctive character of judgment
have upon the problem of interpreting existence? In its very
function of a knowing activity, judgment is dynamic and
synthesizing and conditioned by time. For that reason what
it grasps is expressed and recorded in the synthesis of a proposition and communicated through a sentence. But the activity
of judgment, like any other activity, is specified by its object.
Its knowable character is revealed by the knowable character
of the object. This means that its object, existence, is a synthesizing, dynamic, and temporally conditioned actuality.

Only through knowing these characteristics in the object are we able to attribute them to the activity that apprehends it. In this case the object is the thing's existence. The thing's existence is, accordingly, a synthesizing that is dynamically taking place in time. The synthesizing of passenger pigeons in real existence was occurring a century ago, but it is not occurring now. The synthesizing could then be expressed by the proposition "Passenger pigeons exist." The synthetic form of the proposition mirrored in static fashion a synthesizing that was dynamically taking place in reality. The synthesizing was, in fact, the birds' existence. No longer occurring in the real world, the synthesizing today cannot be the object of the judgment that the birds really exist.

Confronted with what one now judges, the proposition "Passenger pigeons exist" would be immediately characterized as false. But this confrontation of the proposition with the object of the judgment helps to show vividly that what the judgment grasps is a synthesizing that is actually taking place in time. Little wonder, then, that this object can be expressed only in the complexity of a proposition, and not in the simplicity of a single word.

The temporal character of the existential synthesizing, moreover, means that the existence is always *lacking*[6] in what

---

[6] Cf.: "Thus the being of the object is pure non-being. It is defined as a lack. It is that which escapes, that which by definition will never be given, that which offers itself only in fleeting and successive profiles." Jean-Paul Sartre, *Being and Nothingness*, tr. Hazel E. Barnes (New York, 1956), p. lxiii (lxi). "Nothingness lies coiled in the heart of being — like a worm." *Ibid.*, p. 21. Compare Aquinas: "But our existence has some of itself outside itself; for the part of it that has already gone by is lacking, and so is that which is going to be." *In I Sententiarum*, d. 8, q. 1, a. 1, Solut.; ed. Mandonnet, I, 195. Further, "whatever aspect of being anything has, it has only from God; but the deficiency of being is from itself." *In II Sententiarum*, d. 37, q. 1, a. 2, Solut.; II, 946. In view of the fluidity of existence in Aquinas, it would be hard to bring him under the censure: "For the tradition known as *philosophia perennis*, the expression 'historicity of philosophic truth' is a contradiction in terms." Emil Fackenheim, "The History and Transcendence of Philosophic Truth," *Proceedings of the Seventh Inter-American Congress of Philosophy*, I, 79. For Aquinas, truth is expressly founded on existence

pertains to its fullness. It is never complete at any one moment. The existence is in the present, but coming out of the past and going on into the future. It is always present in an instant, but with a part that is past and a part that is future. Yet except for what is there in the instant, the past has ceased to exist and the future does not yet exist. For this reason temporal existence is radically incomplete, potential, and open to progress and development. Pulsating in the present, it is always sloughing the past and plunging into the future. The unceasing gyration of the fundamental particles as well as the relentless outward journeying of the galaxies manifest this condition on the level of physics. The tearing

---

grasped through judgment, and in our world this existence is incessantly changing. See subsequent, nn. 8 and 16. Perhaps the excommunication of Aquinas from the *philosophia perennis* is not something to be mourned. After all, the term is only of Renaissance coinage, and in English the label "perennial" suggests the notion of a plant that comes up in exactly the same way every year. In contrast, Thomism seems to be different in every one of its proponents who is thinking authentically on the philosophical level. On the historical background of the notion, see Hermann Ebert, "Augustinus Steuchus und seine *Philosophia perennis*," *Philosophisches Jahrbuch*, XLII (1929), 342–356; 510–526; XLIII (1930), 92–100: and Charles B. Schmitt, "Perennial Philosophy: from Agostino Steuco to Leibniz," *Journal of the History of Ideas*, XXVII (1966), 505–532.

At *Summa Contra Gentiles*, I, 20, "Procedit," in contrast to the fluid nature of movement, existence is called by Aquinas "*aliquid fixum et quietum in ente*" ("something fixed and transpired in being"). In the preceding context ("Et ideo"), movement had been described as having in its very notion quantity and extension. In contrast, "*Esse autem non habet aliquam extensionem quantitatis: praecipue in re cuius esse est invariabile, sicut caelum*" ("Existence has no quantitative extension: especially in a thing whose existence is invariable, as the heavens"). In a similar context of the discussion with Averroes, St. Thomas, *In VIII Physicorum*, lect. 21, Angeli-Pirotta no. 2488, notes that though the heavenly body has no potency to nonexistence, it has potency to be at rest (*ad quietem*). At *In I Sententiarum*, d. 8, q. 2, a. 1, ad 6m (ed. Mandonnet, I, 203), the term *quies* is used to emphasize the lack of extension in the divine existence, in contrast to the meaning of "duration." At *De Veritate*, XXI, 4, ad 7m, existence is characteristic of God, and through likeness to the divine existence the existence of creatures, though mixed with past and future, receives its designation. These texts indicate clearly enough the meaning that while movement is in its nature fluid, existence is not fluid in its nature but only in temporal instances. On the contrast between changeable and unchangeable existence, see *Summa Theologiae*, I, 10, 5c, and on the Greek background of the truly existent (*enter, vel existenter ens*) as opposed to the changeably existent (*mobiliter ens*), see *In Librum de Causis*, Prop. 2; ed. Saffrey, p. 13.6–12.

apart and building up in the processes of metabolism are without pause on the physiological plane. Psychologically, man never remains satisfied in his temporal existence, and even tends to glory in the malaise that relentlessly urges him on:

> Neither my body nor my soul
>   To earth's low ease will yield consent.
> I praise Thee for my will to strive,
>   I bless Thy goad of discontent.[7]

This, of course, is by no means a denial of the tenet that the natures of things, except those that consist in movement, are essentially stable in character. While the heating of water or the activity of walking are processes by their very nature, things like water, hydrogen, triangularity, the *modus ponens*, remain the same in nature as the centuries glide past. Tower Bridge keeps spanning the Thames; Pike's Peak continues to rise out of the Rockies. A man stays animate throughout the whole course of his life. Yet, existentially, these structural aspects are incessantly changing as they go on from past to future, no matter how stable they are essentially. Whether or not the ever varying existential aspect is more basic and more dominating than the stable essential character is a question that still has to be faced. For the moment, however, it is clear that insofar as the essential aspects exist, they are inevitably subject to unrelenting existential variation.[8] From

---

[7] Charles G. D. Roberts, *The Aim*; in *Selected Poems* (Toronto, 1936), p. 93.

[8] Cf.: "Forms are called invariable because they themselves cannot be the subjects of variation; but . . . they vary in exactly the same way as they exist; for they are said to exist not as subjects of existence, but because things have existence through them." St. Thomas Aquinas, *Summa Theologiae*, I, 9, 2, ad 3m; ed. Blackfriars (London & New York: Eerie & Spottiswode and McGraw-Hill, 1964), II, 133. ". . . time is properly the measure of change. . . . So the existence of perishable things, being changeable, is measured by time . . ." *Ibid.*, I, 10, 4, ad 3m; II, 147. "Now some things fall far enough short of abiding existence to have an existence consisting in or subject to change, and such things time measures; all movements, for example, and in perishable things, even their existence." *Ibid.*, a. 5c; p. 149. See also: *In I Sententiarum*, d. 8, q. 2, a. 2, Solut. (ed. Mandonnet, I, 205); d. 19, q. 2, a. 2, Solut. (I, 470–471). *In Boethii de Trinitate*, V, 2c; ed. Decker, p. 176.7–9.

a metaphysical viewpoint, the ingrained historicity of existence in the real world must require that everything the existence actualizes be thrown into continual change. Existence as apprehended by judgment is a dynamic and fluid synthesizing in time.

The importance of this consideration for the interpretation of existence is obviously fundamental. If existence is approached as though it were originally known through a concept and communicated vocally by means of a single word, it could be regarded as something fixed and finished in itself, a closed and finite nature. The need for understanding it as something ever incomplete, something always opening on novelty, something inevitably reaching out to something else, would be missed. It would be placed on the same level as the essential aspects of the thing, would soon be found to reveal no new content on that plane, and accordingly would be reduced to the role of an auxiliary logical symbol. To open out in the direction in which it may be regarded as somehow holding the spiritual destiny of men, does it not have to be understood from the start in a way that will allow it to reveal its own rich content and irrepressible dynamism?

The insight that existence is originally apprehended through judgment appears first in Thomas Aquinas.[9] The tenet has no visible ancestry, even though an extensive background against which it could emerge had been in a process of development from Parmenides through Plato, Aristotle, and Plotinus to Avicenna and William of Auvergne. But in

[9] "The first operation regards the thing's quiddity; the second regards its being." In I Sententiarum, d. 19, q. 5, a. 1, ad 7m; I, 489. ". . . every incomplex thing has its being, which is not attained by the intellect except in the manner of a complexity." Ibid., p. 490. "The other grasps the being of the thing, composing the affirmation, because also the being of the thing from which it acquires the cognition consists in a certain composition of form with matter, or of accident with subject." Ibid., d. 38, q. 1, a. 3, Solut.; I, 903. "But the second operation regards the very being of the thing, which results from the association of the principles of the thing in composites . . ." In Boethii de Trinitate, V, 3c; ed. Decker, p. 182.9–10.

Aquinas there occurs the discontinuous jump in the evolutionary process and with it the sudden emergence of a radically new way of metaphysical thinking. The background had been prepared by Aristotle in his logical analysis of the proposition, with the distinction of its complex type of knowledge from the simple type of cognition by which the terms were known. It was furthered by the long Christian Neoplatonic tradition, in which existence gradually came to be regarded as the primary characteristic in a thing, and by the Avicennian tenet that existence accrued to the thing's nature and functioned in a way that was described in the Latin translation as accidental to the thing.

Finally, in the immediate background of Aquinas, there was William of Auvergne's clearly stated distinction, and his vigorous assertion of the superiority of existence in respect of anything in the thing's nature.[10] But the genetic leap to judgment as a distinct synthesizing cognition that apprehends an existential synthesizing in the thing appears for the first time in Aquinas. It ushers in a profoundly new metaphysical starting point.

Nor is there any evidence that it was understood or appreciated by his successors. The distinction between simple apprehension and judgment did become a commonplace in Scholastic tradition. But the logical background of the distinction proved too dominant to allow the metaphysical import of the Thomistic texts to make itself felt. Existence came to be regarded in the Thomistic tradition as a reality (res) contrasted with another reality, the thing's essence. Just as the logician takes the subject and predicate as fully constituted terms and then considers the nexus between them, so the *perspicientia nexus* was separated from the judgment, and the judgment was regarded as a rubber-stamp

---

[10] William of Auvergne, *De Trinitate*, cc. II & VII (ed. Orleans & Paris, 1674), II, Suppl. pp. 2b & 9a.

approval or acceptance of what was already perceived. The Thomistic insight that the judgment itself was the original knowledge of the existential synthesis eluded the attention of the later Scholastic thinkers. The notion that the intellectual activity of synthesizing was itself the knowing of existence escaped them.[11]

In Kant's penetrating scrutiny, however, the notion that a synthesis underlies conceptual knowledge reappears: "For where the understanding has not previously combined, it cannot dissolve, since only as having been combined *by the understanding* can anything that allows of analysis be given to the faculty of representation."[12] The synthesizing activity of the human intellect is thereby recognized as prior to the thinking of any notion "in the analytic unity of consciousness, which makes it a *conceptus communis*."[13] With Kant, of course, the synthesizing activity was not the knowing of any *thing in itself*. Yet with him reappears the insight that in human intellectual activity a synthesis always lies deeper than conceptualization. In Bergson the tenet that what is basic in reality itself is a flowing duration beyond the grasp of static intellection is emphasized. In Heidegger the need for "the *preconceptual* understanding of Being"[14] is paramount, and

---

[11] On the general background of this topic, see Etienne Gilson, *Being and Some Philosophers*, 2nd ed. (Toronto: Pontifical Institute of Mediaeval Studies, 1961), pp. 190–232; Peter H. J. Hoenen, *Reality and Judgment according to St. Thomas*, tr. Henry F. Tiblier (Chicago: Henry Regnery, 1952); Francis M. Tyrrell, *The Role of Assent in Judgment* (Washington, D. C.: Catholic University of America, 1948); F. A. Cunningham, "Judgment in St. Thomas," *The Modern Schoolman*, XXXI (1954), pp. 185–212. "The Second Operation and the Assent vs. the Judgment in St. Thomas," *The New Scholasticism*, XXXI (1957), pp. 1–33; Robert W. Schmidt, "The Evidence Grounding Judgments of Existence," in *An Etienne Gilson Tribute*, ed. Charles J. O'Neil (Milwaukee: Marquette University Press, 1959), pp. 228–244. J. Owens, "Diversity and Community of Being in St. Thomas Aquinas," *Mediaeval Studies*, XXII (1960), pp. 257–302.

[12] *Critique of Pure Reason*, B 130; tr. Norman Kemp Smith.

[13] *Ibid.*, B 134, note.

[14] Martin Heidegger, *Kant and the Problem of Metaphysics*, tr. James S. Churchill (Bloomington, Ind.: University of Indiana Press, 1962), p. 233. The German *Seinsverständnis*, however, does not carry any overtones of a

with him the distinction of Being from beings is stated anew without any hint that it had not been forgotten by Aquinas.

Furthermore, in Aquinas, what the judgment grasps is always existential in character, even when a predicate other than existence is asserted. In every case an assertion expresses an existential synthesis. This is clearly and trenchantly expressed in a much quoted passage: "However, the actuality which the verb 'is' principally signifies is the actuality of every form commonly, whether substantial or accidental. Hence, when we wish to signify that any form or act is actually in some subject we signify it through the verb 'is,' either absolutely or relatively; absolutely according to present time, relatively according to other times; . . ."[15] May one accordingly extend the notion of judgment, as knowledge specified by an existential synthesis, to all cases in which a predicate is asserted of a subject?

If the conception of actuality just quoted is in fact correct, will not the existential character of all predication inevitably follow from it? What is grasped in judgment, and signified in a proposition by the copula and in speech by the verb "is," will be a form's actuality, whether the form be substantial or accidental. All the Aristotelian categories are thereby covered. For Aquinas everything originally known through conceptualization finds its actuality in the object that is attained through judgment, that is, in existence. While any substantial or accidental nature is grasped through conceptualization, the actuality of the nature is in every case existential, and is known through judgment. It will be this existential actuality that synthesizes the predicamental nature, whether substantial or accidental, with its subject.

---

synthesizing activity, as does the Latin comprehendit in St. Thomas, In I Sententiarum, d. 38, q. 1, a. 3, Solut. (ed. Mandonnet, I, 903) — "Alia autem comprehendit esse rei, componendo affirmationem, . . ." Text cited above in supra, n. 9.

[15] St. Thomas, In I Perihermeneias, lect. 5, n. 22; tr. Jean T. Oesterle.

What is involved in these tenets? When you say, "The cat is black," the synthesizing of the accidental quality "black" with the individual substance "cat" is the existence of "black" in the subject "cat." Nothing in the nature of a cat requires it to be black, and nothing in the nature of the quality "black" requires it to be in a cat. The synthesizing of the two takes place as a fact in actual existence, without any necessitating essential link on the part of either term. It is a synthesizing conditioned by time and changeable in time, in accord with the norms already considered in respect of existence as grasped through judgment.

If the techniques of the beauty parlor are applicable to cats as well as to humans, there is no reason why a black cat today should not be a blonde tomorrow. With the weasel and the rabbit the physiological processes take care of the situation as the seasons of the year change. In the case of entirely accidental predicates, then, it is not hard to see the point emphasized by Aquinas. The synthesis between the terms does not follow from the nature of either, but is found rather in their actual being, their existence.[16]

---

[16] The being that unites "musician" and "carpenter" in the same individual was designated by Aristotle "being in an accidental sense," and was regarded by him as unable to be the subject matter of any science. See *Metaphysics* Δ 7,1017a7–22; E 2,1026b2–21. The temporal character of the being that is predicated shows it to be accidental from the viewpoint of St. Thomas: ". . . being as signifying the composition of a proposition is predicated accidentally, since composition is made by the intellect with regard to a definite time. Now to exist at this or at that particular time is to be an accidental predicate." *In X Metaphysicorum*, lect. 3, Cathala no. 1982; tr. John P. Rowan. On the other hand, "nothing is more essential to a thing than its existence" — Aquinas, *In I Sententiarum*, d. 8, exp. lae partis textus; ed. Mandonnet, I, 209. For Aquinas' treatment of *esse per accidens* against an Aristotelian background and with Aristotle's examples, see *In V Metaphysicorum*, lect. 9, Cathala nos. 886–894; *In VI Metaphysicorum*, lect. 2, nos. 1173–1189. For Aristotle, accidental being was ruled out of consideration in any scientific treatment, by the very fact that it was accidental. For Aquinas, on the contrary, the accidental characteristic is present in all being that is encountered immediately in the observable world. But at the same time this being has its necessary characteristics, and these necessary characteristics allow the being that is known in sensible things to serve as the starting point for cogent demonstrations in metaphysics.

The problem, however, becomes more difficult in the case of predicates that remain within the category of substance, and in general wherever the predicate is a generic characteristic of the subject. "Socrates is a man," for example, or "Man is an animal," may seem at first sight beyond the need of existential synthesis and above the conditions of time. Yet there is nothing in the nature of "man" that requires it to be found in Socrates. Human nature can be found just as easily apart from Socrates, for instance, in Plato, in Beethoven, in Johnson. Similarly, there is nothing in the nature of "animal" that requires it to be realized in man. Animality can be found equally well apart from man in brutes. The apparent difficulty here lies in the one-sided approach. Socrates is necessarily a man and man is necessarily an animal. But a man is not necessarily Socrates, nor is an animal necessarily a man. To see the requirement for existential synthesizing in this area, one approaches from the more generic or, in the case of the individual, from the specific side.

But be that as it may, unless Socrates existed in some way he would not be a man or anything else, and unless a specific nature existed in some way, it also would not be anything at all. In either case you would have nothing. So, for a subject to be anything at all, in a way that offers the ground for a proposition, existence in its synthesizing function has to be involved. This brings forward the problem of the different ways of existing,[17] and requires a complicated explanation of the way in which essences may be said to be eternally true.[18] These considerations may be deferred for the moment. It is sufficient for the present to note that what is represented by the subject concept is seen to be identified in existence with what is represented by the predicate concept, so that the one *is* the other, e.g., Socrates is a man and man is an animal.

---

[17] See my paper "The Range of Existence," *Proceedings of the Seventh Inter-American Congress of Philosophy* (Quebec, 1967), I, pp. 47–50.

[18] See St. Thomas, *Quodlibetales*, VIII, lc, and ad lm.

The requirement of existence for every predication, no matter what verb is used or predicate asserted, has not gone unnoticed in modern philosophy. It was tellingly emphasized in Bertrand Russell's early explanation of the philosophy of logical atomism: ". . . always this statement of his existence is part of the proposition. . . . So that any statement in which a description has a primary occurrence implies that the object described exists."[19] In the important discussion of Kneale and Moore on existence as a predicate, the presuppositions of existence in every predication came to the fore: "It seems to me that 'This exists' (in this usage) always forms part of what is asserted by 'This is a book,' 'This is red,' etc., where 'this' is used in the manner with which we are now concerned."[20]

A similar notion is expressed by Ayer: "For, when we ascribe an attribute to a thing, we covertly assert that it exists."[21] In this regard perhaps the strongest statement of the case is given by Alston: "Before we can attach any predicate to anything ('round,' 'heavy,' 'in my pocket,' 'belongs to Jones,' 'difficult to understand') we must presuppose that it exists. . . . If the existence of the subject must be presupposed before we can set about attaching (withholding, wondering whether to attach) any predicate to (from) it, we will always be too late either to apply or to withhold a predicate of existence."[22] It could hardly be more strongly stated that existence is a presupposition for predication. From another viewpoint, the same necessary accompaniment of existence in every object of thought is asserted by Hartshorne: " . . . if any thought is not about the existent, I do not know what it is about."[23]

19 "The Philosophy of Logical Atomism," The Monist, XXIX (1919), 218.
20 G. E. Moore, "Is Existence a Predicate?" Proceedings of the Aristotelian Society, Supplement, XV (1936), p. 187.
21 Language, Truth and Logic, 2nd ed. (New York, Dover: 1947), p. 43.
22 William P. Alston, "The Ontological Argument Revisited," The Philosophical Review, LXIX (1960), p. 454.
23 Charles Hartshorne, The Logic of Perfection (LaSalle, Ill.: Open Court Publishing Co., 1962), pp. 84–85.

These modern insights, it is true, do not concern themselves explicitly with the synthesizing character of existence.
But they do stress cogently that existence is presupposed by
and implied in every predication whatsoever. The consequence is that what the judgment grasps is always existence,
no matter what predicate it is asserting. In statements such
as "The cat is frisky," "The rug is yellow," "The motor hums
nicely," "The sentence reads well," "Proximity is a relation,"
or "Two and two are four," the synthesis of predicate with
subject rests on existence. Even though no verb is written
or spoken, as in many assertions made in Latin or Russian,
what is asserted involves in every case the existence of the
predicate in the subject.[24]

But what about things that do not exist in the real world?
Olympian gods, folklore elves, the numerous characters of
fiction, the *modus tollens*, the square root of two, all have
their existence only in the activity of the human mind. But
they do exist in human thought, when anyone is thinking
of them. In that existence one synthesizes characteristics with
subject. Varied traits and activities are accordingly attributed
to fictional or mythological personages. To say, for instance,
that the class of Olympian gods is empty, is not comprehen-
sive enough to meet the issue. One may grant readily that
Olympian gods do not exist in the real world. The question
whether they exist in some other fashion, however, remains
open. If they are found to exist in human thought, they can
hardly form an empty class, unless by a convention of logic
"existence" is restricted arbitrarily to existence in the real

---

[24] E.g., "*Initium sapientiae timor Domini*" (Fear of the Lord [is] the
beginning of wisdom") or in Greek the proverb that in wine there is truth.
In a Slavic language such as Russian the adjective is asserted of the subject
without use of the verb "is" in its version of sentences like "The man is sick."
In English the notions expressed by verbs are in most cases asserted of their
subject without the use of the copula, as in "he runs, he talks." But there are
also forms in which the appropriate part of the verb "to be" is expressed, as
in "he is running, he is talking."

universe. But do they not in point of fact exist in human thought when one is thinking about them? Do they not come into cognitional existence every time one imagines them or discusses them?

It would not be hard to collect numerous instances in which the word "exist" is used in this sense in ordinary language. We say that political tensions exist in Cyprus, that hope still exists for a settlement, that Auschwitz must continue to exist in our memories, that many amusing characters exist in fiction. What we mean is that these objects have come to exist in human minds through the activity of human thinking. They are products of an activity, of efficient causality. It is not just a question of a static relation. A portrait is related to the man it represents; a label is related to the contents of a bottle; a library index card is related to the book about which it gives the data. But would anyone care to say that these relations consist in knowing their respective relata? Have they not a considerably different role in regard to those relata? They may signify them; they may represent them, but they do not know them.

Knowing is of a very different character. True, it sets up a relation between knower and known, but it does not consist in that relation, any more than begetting consists in the relation of fatherhood. Knowing consists rather in the activity that makes something be present in the mind, that is, an activity by which cognitional existence is given to the object known. Correspondingly, being known consists in having that cognitional existence. Knowledge may represent or picture the thing known. But knowledge does not consist in the representing or picturing. To know, basically, means something different from picturing or representing. One type of cognition, external perception, in fact does not represent or picture its object at all. Even where one says that a man exists in his portrait, what one quite obviously means is that

the portrait recalls his features so clearly that it vividly brings
the man into the cognition of anyone who is contemplating
it. Without the activity of the contemplating cognition there
would be no question of the portrait's giving the man existence. As regards the label and the index card, one would
hardly say that what they signify exists in them.

Accordingly, there is no ground for claiming that to exist
only in the imagination means not to exist at all. The correct
expression in that case would be that the object does not
exist even in the imagination. In saying that a thing exists
only in the imagination, one means that it does exist there,
even though it does not exist in the real world.[25] Quite correctly, the phrasing "exists only in the imagination" or "exists
only in thought" implies that cognitional existence is a lesser
type of existence than real existence. To exist in one's own
self in the real world is obviously much more meaningful
than to exist only in someone's imagination. But both are
genuine ways of existing. Neither is a "half-way" stage of
existence at all.[26] Each, though in its own characteristic way,

[25] "So far as these protests simply amount to an *exclusion* of such phrases
'exists in your imagination' (perhaps on the grounds that only real existence is
real existence), they can be safely ignored." W. P. Alston, *art. cit.*, p. 460.
Moore's difficulty in finding meaning in "Some tame tigers do not exist,"
comparable with the meaning in "Some tame tigers exist," disappears when
the two different ways of existing and the distinction of both from the subject
are kept in mind. In both cases the subject, "tame tigers," has existence in
the mind, and, accordingly, is able to function as a subject for predication. In
the one case real existence is denied it; in the other it is asserted of it. "There
are some tame tigers which do not exist" (Moore, *art. cit.*, p. 181) gives good
sense when the "there are" expresses cognitional existence (in fiction or in
imagination) and the "exist" signifies real existence. Of course, someone who
is really existent has to be doing the thinking and, accordingly, cognitional
existence presupposes real existence. But by the very fact that a thing is being
known, it is an object that has cognitional existence. Only by restricting
"existence" to real existence, consequently, is Meinong able to say, "There
is thus not the slightest doubt that what is supposed to be the Object of
knowledge need not exist at all." Meinong, "The Theory of Objects," in
Realism and the Background of Phenomenology, ed. R. M. Chisholm
(Glencoe, Ill.: The Free Press, 1960), p. 81. For Meinong an object may
subsist (*bestehen*) without existing.
[26] For the viewpoint that would be half-way stages, see Quine, *art. cit.*,
Proceedings of the Seventh Inter-American Congress of Philosophy, I, 62. St.

has all the significant difference between existing and not existing. There is no infringement on the principle of excluded middle. Each is a whole-way existence in its own order. If existence is regarded as a logical auxiliary symbol it will, as has been noted,[27] be unable to be shared in various degrees. But when it is understood as a positive perfection originally grasped through judgment, there is no a priori reason why it cannot be found in differing degrees just as other positive characteristics such as beauty and goodness.

In every case it sets a thing apart from nothing, and in that fashion is a whole-way stage of existence. But just as things themselves in each case are more than nothing even though they differ greatly in degrees of perfection, so their existence is correspondingly of different levels and is exercised in different ways, even though in every instance without exception it authentically makes them exist. The objection seems to imply that cognitional existence is a lesser grade of real existence, and is trying unsuccessfully to ape real existence. But cognitional existence is not a grade of real existence at all. It is genuine existence in cognition, and in no way, let alone half-way, is it real existence. It is an authentic existence of a radically different kind.

Another objection to cognitional existence is its immateriality. It is not existence immediately in real matter, but only in cognitional activity. However, from an Aristotelian and

---

Thomas, In I Sententiarum, d. 2, q. 1, a. 1, Contra (ed. Mandonnet), I, 60, uses ens diminutum to signify dependent being in contrast to the independent being of God. This is the comparison of primary to secondary instances of being. The expression is entirely in order where the primary instance is the exemplar cause of the secondary instances and is imitated by them in various degrees. Such for St. Thomas is the case with being; see In I Sententiarum, Prol., q. 1, a. 2, ad 2m (I, 10), and d. 8, q. 1, a. 2 (I, 198). Each instantiation has genuine existence. On the contrary, for Gabriel Marcel, The Philosophy of Existence, tr. Manya Harari (Chicago: Regnery, 1948), p. 23, the "diminution of the object" refers to the effigy itself, not to any new cognitional existence had in it by the object. Accordingly he can speak of "a diminution or an effigy" (ibid., p. 24). For St. Thomas, cognitional existence would always mean "presence" of the object.

[27] See Chapter 1, n. 8.

Scholastic viewpoint, immateriality is the explanation of cognition, and is even looked upon as a higher kind of existence than existence in matter, though with appropriate reservations. Suffice it to say that cognitional existence is indeed immaterial in the Aristotelian understanding of the notion, and by that very fact is cognition. It is not in any way trying to be material, any more than it is trying to be real existence. The objection seems to presuppose that any genuine existence has to be material existence.

More serious is the further objection that in cognitional existence the objects would lack adequate individuation. In the real world, each thing is individuated in its own existential actuality, an actuality that continues the same in its fluid duration throughout a period of time. In regard to things already in real existence, the human mind is observant rather than productive. It has no control over existence that it merely knows. In cognition, however, the mind gives new existence to the thing known. The mind is here productive, efficiently causal. While the thing known remains the same individual that exists in the real world, why can it not be known under different traits in successive acts of cognition? Does not the Mona Lisa, for example, while remaining identically the same portrait, take on a somewhat different individuality in the mind every time it is contemplated? Does it not break into different meaning in different viewers, and different meaning in the same viewer as he contemplates it at different times?

Why can a real thing not remain the same individual when known by different acts of cognition, even though each cognitive act grasps it under different aspects? Surely no single act of cognition need exhaust the practically unfathomable richness of a real individual. Similarly, fictional characters may retain enough basic traits to ensure their individual identity, even though they undergo drastic revision at the hands of different writers, for instance, in the case of Tristan and Isolde. Fundamentally, the same object is meant, all the while that it is built up in different guises as each new act of cognition gives it new existence.

These two ways of existence, real and cognitional, are known by means of different judgments, each radically irreducible to the other. To know whether a thing exists in the external world, you have to "look outside and see."[28] The "look," on the intellectual level, is the judgment that grasps real existence. Correspondingly, to know that one is thinking or feeling or deciding, one has to look in and see. One has to reflect on one's own activities. The inward look also is a judgment, in the technical sense of the term as an intuition of existence. Again, the existence known is real existence, existence of the really occurring activity in oneself. But within the cognitional activity one is aware of the existence it gives the objects known. Reflexively, one judges that they exist in one's cognition. It is this judgment that is the knowledge of cognitional existence. It is a new and different judgment from the judgment by which the thing's real existence is grasped.

Since the two types of existential judgment are so radically irreducible, the knowledge given by the one cannot be the means of reasoning to the existence known by the other. Cognitional existence in human minds cannot be deduced from real existence. There is every reason to think that many things exist in the real world without ever coming under human knowledge. A philosopher may have some hesitation in making a statement of this kind in his own right, but practically he would not be inclined to offer much resistance to the poet's intuition:

Full many a gem of purest ray serene
  The dark unfathomed caves of ocean bear:

_____
[28] W. P. Alston, art. cit., p. 463.

> Full many a flower is born to blush unseen,
> And waste its sweetness on the desert air. (Gray's *Elegy*)

Nor can the real existence of a thing be deduced from the fact that it has cognitional existence in one's mind. Here the philosopher is on surer ground for making his own assertion. Has he not been forced in his work to ponder over the epistemological problems raised by the Skeptics and by Descartes, about things mistakenly judged to exist in reality when only their existence in illusions, hallucinations, or dreams was actually grasped? Has he himself not enjoyed daydreams that never came true? Does he need any help at all from the poet to know that:

> The best-laid schemes o' mice an' men
> Gang aft agley? (Burns, *To a Mouse*)

In both cases, accordingly, one needs an original judgment of existence to ground any reasoning to further existence, respectively, within the one or the other sphere.

In conclusion, one may say that existence, whether real or cognitional, in every case is grasped through a synthesizing act of cognition that for convenience may be called judgment, in a technical sense of the term. In this type of cognition the synthesizing is the knowing, and the knowing is the synthesizing. The reason the very knowing is a synthesizing is that the existence itself is a synthesizing actuality requiring apprehension in corresponding fashion. In consequence it demands authentic expression in a proposition rather than in a concept, and communication not through a word but through a sentence.

Finally, the importance of understanding how existence is originally grasped by the human mind can hardly be overstressed in problems about its interpretation. If existence is approached as though it were something originally known by means of a concept, it will eventually turn out to be totally empty of content. Its meaning in reality will become a haze.

This consequence has been shown over and over again in modern philosophy. Existence, accordingly, will be reduced to the role of a logical auxiliary symbol. It will not be an actuality susceptible of different degrees; it will not appear as something radically incomplete and opening on further vistas. Once it is clearly understood, however, as an actual synthesizing that is grasped through a distinctive act of intellection, namely judgment, it offers enticing prospects. It will appear as a challenging actuality in the thing known, the actuality that sets the thing apart from nothing. Its temporal conditioning and incompleteness, its capacity to make a thing exist on two different levels, real and cognitional, its fluid character that refuses to be compressed into the confines of a static concept, all pose problems that promise rich results if they are adequately investigated.

What one has to do, then, is carefully to reflect on one's own experience of knowing that things exist. If one finds that in every case one knows this through an act of judgment, one will be bearing out in one's own investigation the observations of the present chapter. One will have isolated a distinctive type of cognition through which is offered a sufficient starting point for profitable inquiry into an obvious aspect of the universe that, according to Heidegger's suggestion, may hold on the philosophical level "the spiritual destiny of the West."

CHAPTER III

Characteristics of Existence

The assurance that existence is originally grasped through the synthesizing act of judgment leaves one unperturbed at the charges of emptiness in its concept. Existence manifests a very distinctive content when it is assessed as the object of judgment, and not of conceptualization. But this is a content that is studded with difficulties as well as with challenge. First of all, how can it be characterized in any way? To be regarded as having characteristics by which it may be described in itself and in distinction from other objects, it clearly has to be the subject of predication. The characteristics have to be predicable of it. Without universal characteristics that can function as middle terms in a reasoning process, how could the content of existence enable the human intellect to draw any meaningful conclusions from it? Would not the intellect be confined in its regard to the mere stating of a fact, known definitely through judgment, but utterly sterile in respect of any further understanding or penetration of its meaning?

Certainly as grasped through judgment existence does not have the role of a subject. In this perspective it is a predicate only. It is asserted of something else. Tables and typewriters, pens and pencils, trees and stones exist. That is what one knows through judgment. Through it, existence is always grasped as a predicate. Never through judgment is existence attained as a subject of predication. To function as the subject of predication, it obviously has to be conceptualized and represented as "something" that has this or that characteristic.

How can the conceptualization take place? That things exist is grasped through judgment by the intellect as a fact, and communicated through a sentence. But the fact that these things exist may then be referred to as their "existence," expressed by a single word. Does this indicate that what was known dynamically through judgment is now being frozen into a concept? Everything points that way. What is referred to as existence is made to function as the subject of propositions, and various predicates are applied to it. It has the role of a topic for study in discussions about it.

One says that existence is difficult to deal with in philosophy, that existence is a hoary problem in analysis, that existence is empty of content. Uses of the notion such as these have been made frequently in the two preceding chapters. No longer is a dynamic predicative function assigned to existence, but rather the static role of notions such as whiteness, power, or essence. This means that what was originally known through judgment is now being represented in a concept. Instead of a fluid and synthesizing predicate, it appears in a new role in which it functions with all the stability and self-contained definiteness that the intellect gives an object when conceiving it. Do not these considerations show beyond any doubt that the human mind does form a concept of existence when it thinks about and investigates what it originally knows through judgment?

But how is such a concept formed? Obviously, it is representing in a conceptualized fashion what was already known dynamically through judgment. On the surface, there is no extraordinary problem in this. What the intellect knows in one way it can represent in other ways. What it knows as a desk it can represent as an artifact, as a corporeal object, as a qualification of a substance. It can use other and more generic concepts to represent what it grasps specifically. But all these generic determinations in the categories are themselves known originally through conceptualization. They are authentic concepts of the things, when the things are considered in broader perspectives. Known specifically through concepts, things like stones and metals and trees and men readily can be represented under their more generic aspects.

Existence, however, is not known originally through any concept whatsoever. There simply is no original characteristic concept of existence that could be broadened out into generic aspects upon confrontation with other objects. One does not have the same type of starting point with existence as one has with objects that come under the categories. In this case the generic aspects will have to be taken from things known originally through conceptualization, and applied to what is known in another way, namely through judgment. Accordingly, the concept will not arise out of the object originally known, as it arises for instance in the case of the generic notion "animal" that is found in man and brute when they are confronted with each other. Can any concept of existence, then, be called authentic, if it has to arise from some object other than the one known through judgment? Can it be anything else than empty, from the viewpoint of what characteristically pertains to existence?

The situation bristles with difficulties. The broadest and most extensive notion found in objects belonging to the categories is that of "thing" or "something." Whatever goes in any of the categories can be referred to, not exactly generically, but rather, supergenerically, as "something." In this sense a stone is something, a man is something, a quantity is something, a color is something, a relation is something. This supergeneric concept of "something" is derived clearly enough from things that go in the categories. Clearly enough it is an authentic concept, originating through conceptualization of these things under their widest and all-extensive aspect. It has its own content, vague but genuine, the content that enables one to call its object a thing in the broadest sense of that multifaceted term.

Is one permitted, then, to extend the notion "something" to represent what is known through judgment? In ordinary thought, one does so as a matter of course. One says, for instance: "That racial tensions exist is something that cannot be overlooked." What is known through the existential synthesis is taken up again under the concept of "something." Existence, accordingly, may be referred to as "something" that is difficult to investigate, and its synthesizing may be called "something" that is taking place in the real or cognitional world. There seems to be little difficulty, then, in extending the concept "something" to cover any object of cognition, even when the object is known originally not through conceptualization but through judgment.

As may be suspected, however, considerable therapy is needed. The concept "something" arises from the things in the categories. To bring existence under its range, it is forced to represent existence as a thing, as an object that could be placed in a category. This condition has to be denied in the case of existence. Existence does not become assessed as a thing, even though it is represented as a thing. Actually, there is no special difficulty here. Any of the categories, to serve as a subject of predication and to be discussed or investigated, has to be represented as a substance. "White," for instance, is known originally as a quality that is predicated of a substance, as in the assertion "The golf ball is white." Yet it may be represented as something in itself, namely "whiteness," and discussed and compared with other colors. In representing it in this way in cognitional existence as a substance, one does not for a moment intend to imply that it is a substance. Rather, the human way of thinking requires that all categories other than substance be represented as substances whenever one wishes to think about them separately and discuss them.[1] Thereby one is in no way compelled to think that they are substances.

Similarly, when one talks about existence, one has to represent it as a thing and as a substance, without thereby being required to think that it is a thing or a substance. The extension of the notion "something" to cover existence, therefore, has to take place without implying that existence is a thing. If "something," though taken solely from the realm of the categories, is extended to cover any knowable object whatever, it may be applied to the object known through judgment, on condition that its original connotation of an object belonging to the categories be dropped.

But is this kind of abstraction possible? Certainly it is not abstraction in the same sense in which successive determinations are left out of consideration as one scales the Porphyrian tree. In Socrates one abstracts successively from individuating traits, from the aspects of rational, sensitive, living, corporeal, and, in some nonunivocal way, from substance. All one has left is the content of "something," applicable to all the other categories as well. But from that content one can no longer abstract in the same way. It is an absolutely minimal content that has to remain. It has to be applied just as it is. Even when one regards the notion "object of cognition" as wider

---

[1] Cf.: "And we think we know each thing more fully, when we know what it is, e.g., what man is or what fire is, rather than when we know its quality, its quantity, or its place; since we know each of these predicates also, only when we know what the quantity or the quality is." Aristotle, *Metaphysics*, Z 1,1028a36–b2; Oxford tr.

than "thing" because it is applicable to existence as contradistinguished from thing, one is not thereby continuing the abstractive process. Rather, one is viewing *things* as objects of *cognition*, and in this way is referring what is known through conceptualization to cognitive activity in general. The content of the notion "something" is being carried over, and it remains exactly the same, but it is now used to represent the object of cognition in general instead of the object merely of conceptualization.

In this use, accordingly, the concept of "something" retains all the content it has as object of conceptualization. How, then, is the connotation of belonging to the categories to be dropped? That one does in fact drop the connotation is easy enough to verify. Existence is regarded as something, and then the reservation is made that it does not belong to any of the categories, that it is not originally an object of conceptualization. What is being done? Is not existence being regarded first as "something" from the viewpoint in which "something" functions as an object of cognition, with the notion extended analogously to the object of a cognitive activity different from conceptualization? Does not the analogy run: "As 'something' describes the most general object of conceptualization, so may it be used correspondingly for existence insofar as the latter has the role of object of judgment"? In this analogous fashion "something" is extended to cover the object of cognition in general. But if in this further application the content of the concept "something" remains the same, how can the connotation of belonging to the categories be eliminated?

The answer, as should be quite clear from what already has been considered about the process employed by the reflecting intellect, is not to be sought in conceptualization, but rather in judgments formed about the object conceptualized. Existence is represented conceptually as "something." Then it is judged not to be something in the categories or something known originally through conceptualization. In a word, these characteristics are *separated* from it through acts of judgment. The process may be called separation[2] in contradistinction to abstraction, when abstraction is limited to the conceptual process of merely leaving certain traits out of consideration. Here the content of "something" remains integrally in the notion of object of cognition, but the distinctive characteristics of it as the object of conceptualization are regarded as deliberately separated from it through judgment. Correspondingly, a relation, say fatherhood, may be represented as a substance in order to function as a subject of discussion, while at the same time one judges that fatherhood is not a substance but a relation.

There is, however, a difference. One has an original, authentic concept of a relation. One does not have this type of concept in regard to existence. What kind of a concept, then, is reached when one has only the above analogous method at one's service? The concept has no positive content that in itself extends outside the categories. Nothing arising from its own content is common to both itself and what is grasped through judgment. Accordingly, no authentically conceptual note may contain the meaning of existence. When "authentic" is taken in the etymological sense that implies an original source for something, there can be no authentic concept here. Nothing in the concept is the original source of one's knowledge of existence. All the content in the *concept* of existence comes from a different sphere, from the categories. Only by the reflection that existence is positively known, and that

---

[2] Cf.: "Consequently, the consideration of substance without quantity belongs to the order of separation rather than to that of abstraction . . . the operation of the intellect joining and dividing which is properly called separation; and this belongs to divine science or metaphysics." St. Thomas Aquinas, *The Divisions and Methods of the Sciences*, (*In Boethii de Trinitate*), V, 3; tr. A. Maurer, 3rd revised ed. (Toronto: Pontifical Institute of Mediaeval Studies, 1963), pp. 33–34. See Robert W. Schmidt, "L'emploi de la séparation en métaphysique," *Revue Philosophique de Louvain*, LVIII (1960), pp. 373–393.

whatever is positively known may be referred to as "something," in this case through the analogy of the two cognitive acts, is existence represented in the concept. But the whole content of the concept remains outside the existential order. That this typewriter exists is known originally and authentically only through judgment. Nothing of conceptual origin can give rise to that knowledge.

These considerations explain how the *concept* of existence can be regarded as empty. If one is looking for new and original conceptual knowledge in it, there is none to find. It is the concept of a thing, as a thing is found in the categories and is known through conceptualization. Nothing over and above the objects in the categories appears when the concept is analyzed just in itself. When a conceptual element over and above the nonexistential content is sought, the result is entirely a blank.

These reflections likewise apply to the pronouns that refer to existence. In the preceding discussions, "it" and the relative "what" have been frequently used to carry the notion. Existence is *what* is grasped through judgment, and *it* is expressed in a proposition. The pronouns represent existence as a thing that can be thought about and discussed. They have, accordingly, the same force as "something" from the standpoint of the conceptualization of existence.

But is there not a more specific notion available for the conceptual representation of existence? When existence is considered in relation to the thing it makes exist, it may be regarded as actualizing the thing and, accordingly, it appears as the actuality that gives the thing existence. The term "actuality" (*energeia*) had been coined by Aristotle to express the role of the formal elements in the thing.[3] What is formal

[3] For a study of the texts, see George A. Blair, "The Meaning of 'Energeia' and 'Entelecheia' in Aristotle," *International Philosophical Quarterly*, VII (1967), pp. 101–117. Despite his rather provocative conclusion that "the traditional meaning 'actuality' is wrong no matter which word it applies to" (p.

actuates its subject. Analogously what is known through judgment actuates the composite of form and matter. The notion "actuality" was therefore at hand to express conceptually what is known through judgment. Moreover, it offered means for describing existence in a way that distinguished existence from any other kind of actuality.

Since the actuality grasped through judgment is what actualizes all the formal elements in the thing, including its activities, and these formal aspects and activities embrace all the actuality in the thing besides existence, existence appears, accordingly, as the actuality of all actualities. This is saying merely that without existence a thing is nothing. Without existence none of its formal elements or activities are actual. To be actual, these have to exist. Though by definition they are actualities, they attain this status only through existing. In a word, they cannot be actual as their nature requires unless they are actuated by existence. In this way, by remaining within the one analogous notion of actuality, existence may be accurately described as the actuality that actualizes all other actualities.[4]

An alternate word for actuality in this respect is "perfection" (entelecheia). It was used by Aristotle along with actuality to designate the formal elements in the thing. These perfected the material element in the sense of filling its potentiality and completing the thing. Since existence is required to complete the thing and all the formal elements and

---

116), the writer concedes that every use of entelecheia is paralleled somewhere in Aristotle by a use of energeia "in exactly the same sense" (p. 102). Cf. ibid., p. 110. For present purposes, the two terms may be taken as synonymous. Aristotle's notion that a real form was actual of itself, and not through any further existential actuality, is sufficient to explain why "activity" can be read into his philosophical uses of energeia. But surely activity is everywhere an actuality.

[4] Cf.: ". . . being is the actuality of every form or nature; for goodness or humanity is not signified in actuality except insofar as we signify that it exists." St. Thomas Summa Theologiae, I, 3, 4, ad 2m. ". . . what I call being is the actuality of all actualities, and consequently is the perfection of all perfections." De Potentia, VII, 2, ad 9m. See also Chapter II, n. 15.

activities, it may be aptly called the perfection of all perfections. The analogous application of the term "perfection" in
this case follows the same process as in the case of "actuality."
Again it describes existence accurately while remaining within
the ambit of a single analogous notion.

However, there is still a problem. Even though the notions
of actuality and perfection can be developed in a way that
describes existence accurately in the sense of distinguishing
it sharply from all else, do they succeed in bringing any new
and characteristic content into the concept of existence? Certainly the notions of actuality and perfection as philosophical
concepts were taken originally from the realm of the categories. They express a feature pertaining to the essences of things.
By analogy they may be carried over to the existential order
— as form actualizes and perfects matter, so does existence
actualize and perfect a thing. The notions of actuality and
perfection are thereby extended to designate what is known
through judgment. But no new conceptual content is added
in the process. Nothing characteristic of existence enters into
the concept. The whole content remains what was taken
from the categories. The content now can be focused on what
is known through judgment and used to represent it in a way
that distinguishes it from all other actuality and perfection.
But in itself, apart from being focused on what is grasped
through judgment, the content of the concept does not convey what is characteristic of the object of judgment, namely
that something exists.

The answer to the question of the preceding paragraph,
therefore, must be negative. To conceive existence in terms
of actuality or perfection is not to bring anything new or
characteristic into the concept. While reference to existence
as "something," or as an "it" or a "what" leaves the notion
vague and common to all other things, the description as
the actuality of all actualities or the perfection of all perfec-

tions pinpoints the concept to what is grasped through judgment. But nothing characteristically existential enters into the content. In this sense there is still not even the beginning of an authentic or genuine or, if an obsolete Latinism may be pardoned for the moment, a "proper" concept of existence.

That something exists also may be called a fact. The reference, as the etymology shows, is to the product of an activity. It means something made or done. The content of the notion, accordingly, does not go outside the ambit of the categories. Moreover, the term "fact" is regularly limited to what is observed, in contrast to inferences and conclusions. To make "fact" the typical philosophic term for what is meant in saying that a thing exists would be to exclude any possible role of a starting point for establishing the existence of anything unobservable. But this possibility has to be left open in the framework sketched for the present inquiry in its opening chapter. Only after a close investigation may the decision be given on one side or the other. To use "facticity" or "factuality"[5] as entirely synonymous with "existence" would be to weigh the scales heavily in favor of complete philosophic blankness for the existential dimension. The fallout from the logical attack would spread into metaphysical terrain the notion of existence as "essentially a property of a propositional function,"[6] or as "a value of a bound variable."[7]

From either of the two opposite viewpoints, however, the

---

[5] Both these rather difficult terms are recognized by *Webster's Third New International Dictionary* (1964).

[6] Bertrand Russell, "The Philosophy of Logical Atomism," *The Monist*, XXIX (1919), p. 195. See critique by G. E. Moore, "Is Existence a Predicate?" *Proceedings of the Aristotelian Society*, Supplement, XV (1936), pp. 184–185.

[7] "To be is, purely and simply, to be the value of a variable." W. V. Quine, "On What There Is," *The Review of Metaphysics*, II (1948), no. 5, p. 32. Cf.: " 'To be is to be the value of a bound variable.' This I shall call Quine's thesis, . . ." Jaakko Hintikka, "Existential Presuppositions and Existential Commitments," *The Journal of Philosophy*, LVI (1959), p. 128. The wording is changed in Quine's *From a Logical Point of View* (Cambridge, Mass.: Harvard University Press, 1953), p. 13: "To be assumed as an entity . . . be reckoned as . . ."

mere concept of "fact" is not enough just by itself to convey the message that something does exist. One has to assert that the existence of the thing in question *is* a fact. The object of a judgment has to enter the picture. The concept of fact can again be used to take up this knowledge. The case is the same here as with the other terms already considered. The whole content of the concepts denoted by them is from the order of the categories and cannot of itself be the bearer of any authentically existential knowledge.

Even less appropriate than the term "fact" to signify existence is the term "occurrence." Its etymological sense of "running toward" or "running up to" signifies vividly the emergence of something before one's intellectual gaze. The notion clearly originates in a category, the category of action. Only by analogy is the concept extended to the existential realm, and with the restrictions noted in the cases of the previously considered notions. It quite deliberately confines the range of existence to temporal emergence. It would hardly leave open the possibility of extending the concept to existence that does not occur but has abided eternally. That possibility should not be ruled out a priori.

Similar observations may be made in regard to terms like "take place" or "arise" as synonyms for "coming into existence." Their origin is clearly from the realm of the categories. They express becoming, or coming into existence, under the aspect of motion rather than of existence itself. But they do emphasize strongly the temporal character of the existence immediately grasped by the human intellect in things. This existence is fluid and incomplete at any given moment. Temporality and the accompanying incompleteness are striking characteristics of the existence that confronts the human intellect's gaze.

Bound up with the characteristic of temporal fluidity is, as we saw in the preceding chapter, the synthetic aspect of existence. The existence immediately grasped by the intellect is a synthesizing that is taking place in time. The notion of synthesis or synthesizing obviously is taken from the categories. Like the other notions already considered, it is extended by analogy to the existential order. Just as a complex chemical compound is synthesized from elements or simpler compounds, so the essential and accidental constituents of a thing are synthesized through the placing of a thing in itself, that is, through its existence. Here it is quite obvious that no original notion of synthesizing arises immediately from what is known through judgment.

The simple knowledge that cats exist, mats exist, or men exist does not give the concept of a synthesis. Rather, only through complicated philosophical reasoning is the notion of a synthesizing reached in this case.[8] In propositions of the type, "Cats are black," in which accidental attributes are asserted of a subject, the requirements for a synthesis stand

---

[8] Cf.: "For example, when I say, 'Socrates is a man,' the truth of this enunciation is caused by combining the form *humanity* with the *individual matter* by means of which Socrates is *this* man; and when I say, 'Man is white,' the cause of the truth of this enunciation is the combining of whiteness with the subject. It is similar in other cases." St. Thomas, *In IX Metaphysicorum*, lect. 11, no. 1898; tr. J. P. Rowan. Evidently enough, considerable philosophic reasoning lies back of these notions of synthesis.
In the Cathala-Spiazzi edition, the lines immediately preceding the above passage seem to provide for the composition of generic and specific natures both in the object and in the activity of judgment: ". . . *ipsa compositio formae ad materiam, aut eius quod se habet per modum formae et materiae, vel etiam compositio accidentis ad subiectum, . . .*" (". . . the very composition of the form with the matter, or of what serves as the form with the matter, or even the composition of an accident with a subject . . .") *Ibid.* Cf. "*Licet enim genus praedicabile non sit materia, sumitur tamen a materia, sicut differentia a forma. Dicitur enim aliquid animal ex eo quod habet naturam sensitivam. Rationale vero ex eo, quod habet rationalem naturam, quae se habet ad sensitivam sicut forma ad materiam*" ("For although a predicable genus is not matter, nonetheless it is derived from matter, as difference is derived from form. For something is called animal from the fact that it has a sensitive nature. But it is called rational from the fact that it has a rational nature, which is related to the sensitive nature as form to matter"). *In V Metaphysicorum*, lect. 22, no. 1123. However, Cornelio Fabro, *La Nozione Metafisica di Partecipazione*, 2nd ed. (Turin, 1950), pp. 215–216, interprets the insert as meaning the real composition of essence and the actuality of being.

out more clearly. "Black" is joined to "cats" by the copula. But even here the notion that in reality the quality "black" is being synthesized with the substance "cat" has to be inferred. It does not immediately impinge itself upon the mind from what is grasped in judgment. What is grasped in judgment is that cats are black in many instances. The "are" does not at once give rise to the concept of a synthesis. The concept has to be reasoned to analogously on the basis of a content taken entirely from the realm of the categories.

Still more difficult is the notion that the existence itself is being synthesized with the thing, in both the above cases. From this viewpoint existence is at once a synthesizing and a perfection that is thereby synthesized. This clearly is a tenet that is not immediately given, but has to be inferred through careful reasoning. It enables one to speak of a thing receiving existence, of its entering into composition with its existence, of its remaining distinct from its existence. In all these perspectives thing and existence are regarded as two terms contrasted with each other and entering into union with each other. Yet one of the terms, existence, is the synthesizing. It is both the synthesizing and one of the terms synthesized. A remote parallel may be seen in Aristotle's tenet that a thing's form unites the material elements and is thereby its own union with them.[9] Correspondingly the existence is its own union with the thing it makes exist, as well as the union of the thing's essential and accidental constituents. No infinite regress is set up, as would be the case if existence as a perfection required a further existential synthesizing to unite it with the thing.

Another characteristic of existence that protrudes sharply from the discussion in the preceding chapter is its priority in respect of all other features in the thing. This characteristic emerges from the considerations that existence is implied

_____
[9] See Aristotle, *Metaphysics*, Z 17,1041b11–27.

in every assertion, and is presupposed in the attaching or with-holding of any predicate,[10] and is the actuality of every form whether substantial or accidental.[11] If existence is not presup-posed, you do not have anything at all. You have nothing. Every other perfection, accordingly, has to presuppose exis-tence. You may reason to the consideration that a nature can have either real or cognitional existence, and that therefore of itself it is not bound to either. It abstracts from both. But this is only a conclusion reached by the mind. There *is* no such thing as a nature in its absolute consideration. Nature taken absolutely abstracts from all *being* whatsoever. It can-not be found in reality; it cannot be represented distinctively as such in the mind. In either case it would thereby receive existence, real existence in the outside world, cognitional ex-istence in the mind. In stating that a nature in its absolute consideration abstracts from both real and cognitional being, one is not thereby assigning to it a third or existentially neutral way of being. One is assigning no being to it at all, but merely concluding that of itself the nature does not possess any being whatever.[12] Without the presupposition of existence, there cannot be anything else. In this important and unqualified sense, existence is prior to thing and to all formal aspects in the thing.

Accordingly, every other aspect in the thing presupposes existence. An individual can be a man without being Socrates, and an animal without being a man. All other categorical aspects could be eliminated in turn, each one always leaving some other nature that could take its place as an object of consideration. If it is not a quantity, it could be a quality or

[10] See Chapter II, nn. 19–24.
[11] See n. 4, and Chapter II, n. 15.
[12] Discussions of this topic may be found in my articles, "Common Nature: A Point of Comparison between Thomistic and Scotistic Metaphysics," *Mediaeval Studies*, XIX (1957), pp. 1–14; "Thomistic Common Nature and Platonic Idea," *ibid.*, XXI (1959), pp. 211–223; "Unity and Essence in St. Thomas Aquinas," *ibid.*, XXIII (1961), pp. 240–259.

a relation. No one of these categorical aspects is absolutely indispensable for constituting an object that can be known.
But eliminate existence, and nothing whatever is left for
consideration. While other perfections have to be present for
a more or less limited division of things, existence is required
for every one of them. This shows that existence is the most
basic perfection of all in things.[13] In the things of which one
is immediately aware no existence, of course, can be had without a nature that it makes exist. But no one of these natures
is indispensable. Some other nature could be substituted for
it, and there would still be an existent. In no case, however,
would there be anything if the characteristic of existence were
lacking. No other characteristic could be substituted for existence and still leave an object which is capable of being
considered in itself.

A further important characteristic of existence comes to
the fore when one examines more closely the way in which
existence is known. The nature of a thing is what is known
through conceptualization, and in no case among observable
objects does this nature reveal the existence of a thing. The
existence is known only through another and different intellectual activity, judgment. From that standpoint existence
does not manifest itself as part of the thing's nature, or as
contained in some implicit way within that nature. If it were
contained within the thing's nature, its all-embracing scope
would bring everything else into the real unity of that one
single thing, as the reasoning of Parmenides has shown. Existence contained within the nature would render impossible
any generic, specific, or individual distinction of the nature

---

[13] On the argument that being is the last residue in the process of analysis
and is therefore naturally prior, see St. Thomas, *In I Sententiarum*, d. 8,
q. 1, a. 3, "*Praeterea, illud quod est ultimum*" ("Moreover, that which is
ultimate"); ed. Mandonnet, I, 199. Though occurring in an *argumentum in
contrarium*, the reasoning seems conceded in the reply ad 3m, p. 201: "*sed
tamen secundum intentionem, ens est simplicius et prius aliis*" ("Nonetheless
in intention being is more simple and is prior to others"). See also *Summa
Contra Gentiles*, II, 21, Adhuc effectus.

from anything else.[14] Like a juggernaut, existence within a thing's nature would crush any distinction that it touched.

This means that existence is accidental to all observable things, in the important sense that it is not part of their nature. This tenet is correct and far-reaching in its consequences. But it has to be balanced by what in this case is a complementary tenet, the tenet that nothing is more essential to a thing than its existence.[15] Without existence a thing would not even be a thing. It would be nothing, the opposite of thing. For instance, a man is necessarily an animal, he is necessarily a living thing, a corporeal thing, a substance, a being. It is his existence that makes him a being. He could not be a man without being an animal, but just as cogently he could not be an animal or a man unless he were a being. If he is a being, he has some kind of existence, either real or cognitional. The aspect of being is, accordingly, necessary for the object man.

Existence, then, is both accidental and necessary in every observable thing.[16] In the case of existence these two characteristics are not mutually exclusive. Somewhat as the distinction between analytic and synthetic judgments has been shown to be a dogma that is not always airtight in its application,[17] so a close consideration in the present case establishes the mutual compatibility of the necessary and the accidental aspects of existence in respect of observable things. A table

[14] See St. Thomas, *De Ente et Essentia*, c. IV, ed. Roland-Gosselin, p. 34.16–29; tr. A Maurer (Toronto: Pontifical Institute of Mediaeval Studies, 1949), p. 46. Cf. *In I Sententiarum*, d. 8, q. 4, a. 1, ad 2m; I, pp. 219–220. On the way in which the unique subsistent existence is the existence of other things, see Gerald B. Phelan, "The Being of Creatures," *Proceedings of the American Catholic Philosophical Association*, XXXI (1957), pp. 118–125.
[15] See Chapter II, n. 16.
[16] A discussion of the Thomistic texts on this topic may be found in my paper "The Accidental and Essential Character of Being in the Doctrine of St. Thomas Aquinas," *Mediaeval Studies*, XX (1958), pp. 1–40.
[17] See W. V. Quine, *From a Logical Point of View* (Cambridge, Mass.: Harvard University Press, 1953), pp. 20–37.

has to be an artifact. If it were not an artifact, it would not be a table in the literal sense of the word. Similarly, it has to be a composite of matter and form. Unless it were that, it could have no size and no perceptible qualities — it could not be table. Just as necessarily, however, does it have to possess the status of a being. If it were not a being, it would not be a table. But existence is what makes it a being. Existence is, accordingly, necessary for a thing to be a table or anything else, and the existence may be either real or cognitional. But in the one way or the other the thing has to exist if it is to be anything at all. Existence is an absolutely necessary requirement for any other actual perfection.

On the other hand, the accidental character of an observable thing's existence is fully as obvious. The table acquired its existence through the work of the cabinetmaker. It did not, from this viewpoint, have its existence because of any necessity in its nature, but only because of the freely undertaken labor of an artisan. Similarly, it can lose its existence. It can be burned or chopped to pieces. Rather than necessarily belonging to it, its existence is quite precarious. Existence is not part of its nature, and from this standpoint is not absolutely required by its nature. An observable thing's existence is accidental to it from one viewpoint, though absolutely necessary for it from another.

There is no contradiction here. Rather, existence as grasped by the judgment requires these two viewpoints. As prior and most basic, as the actuality of all other actualities in the thing, it has to be there in logical priority before there can be anything else. From this viewpoint it is absolutely necessary for any other perfection in the observable thing. But as originally grasped through judgment, it is not known as part of the thing's nature. What is in the thing's nature is known through conceptualization. The existence, consequently, is originally known as something accidental to the nature. In this cognitional framework no surprise need be occasioned when the accidental character of the existence is verified through destruction or death.

As conceptualized, existence manifests itself as absolutely necessary for the constitution of the thing. As originally grasped through judgment, it shows itself to be accidental to the thing. Existence is that way. It has both aspects, and allows itself to be known under both. If either aspect is neglected or excluded, a one-sided picture arises. If the specific role of judgment is not understood, the contingent side of existence is disregarded as irrelevant to philosophy, for instance in Aristotle and Duns Scotus. If the universalizing and necessitating function of conceptualization is set aside in the case of existence, the extreme individualism and antinomian vagaries of recent existentialist movements result. Existence, as actually found in things, is both highly individual and necessarily specified by a universalizing nature that it actuates. For a balanced estimate, neither viewpoint, neither cognitional approach, can afford to be neglected.

The combined presence of necessary and accidental aspects in existence sets up in consequence a rather different situation from the compatibility of the two aspects in the Aristotelian notion of a property. For Aristotle a property "is a predicate which does not indicate the essence of a thing, but yet belongs to that thing alone, and is predicated convertibly of it. Thus it is a property of man to be capable of learning grammar."[18] But ability to learn grammar, like any other ability to do something, is a predicamental accident belonging to the second division of the Aristotelian category of quality. Yet in the Topics property is contradistinguished from accident. Later tradition expressed this contrast by saying that something could be a predicamental accident and yet a predicable property, in accordance with developments of the notions

18 Topics, I, 5,102a18–20.

of predicaments and predicables. In this setting, however, one is obliged to concede rather that existence is a predicable accident. Nor can one in any way allow that it is a predicamental or categorical notion. It is outside the essence in a way that is crucially different from the situation in regard to a property. A property flows from the essence and is something that follows upon the essence. Existence, on the contrary, is presupposed by the essence and is prior to the essence. The combination of necessary and accidental aspects is, accordingly, of different character in the two situations.[19]

These considerations, consequently, show why existence should not be called a "property" of a thing. It is not something that follows upon a thing's nature, but is prior to the nature. For the same reason there is difficulty in applying the term "attribute" to existence. "Attribute" suggests that the thing is already there and that something else is being attributed to it. But without existence the thing would not be there to receive the attribution. It might not, however, be too much to regard the term "attribute" as extending to whatever can be said about a subject, whether presupposed by the subject or following upon the subject. In this way there is no hesitation in referring to existence also as a "predicate."[20]

As a final characteristic of existence, its distinction from thing or essence may be noted. The distinction has been

---

[19] On the combination of the two in general, see J. Maritain, "Reflections on Necessity and Contingency," in Essays on Thomism, ed. Robert E. Brennan (New York, 1942), p. 33. Cf. "Nothing indeed is so contingent that it does not have some necessary aspect in itself." St. Thomas, Summa Theologiae, I, 86, 3c.

The necessary aspect of existence that is conceded to individuals appears quite strikingly in Russell's attack: ". . . if there were such a thing as this existence of individuals that we talk of, it would be absolutely impossible for it not to apply, and that is the characteristic of a mistake." Bertrand Russell, "The Philosophy of Logical Atomism," The Monist, XXIX (1919), p. 206.

[20] Cf.: ". . . the verb 'is' itself is sometimes predicated in an enunciation, as in 'Socrates is.' . . . Sometimes, however, 'is' is not predicated as the principal predicate, . . . as in 'Socrates is white.' . . . Hence, in such enunciations 'is' is predicated as added to the principal predicate." St. Thomas, In II Perihermeneias, lect. 2, no. 2; tr. Jean T. Oesterle.

mentioned repeatedly in the preceding discussions. In the
framework already developed, it can best be described as the
distinction between what is originally known through conceptualization and what is originally known through judgment. What is originally known through conceptualization is
the thing itself and its categorical traits. What is originally
grasped through judgment is the thing's existence. So understood, this distinction is made upon the basis of one's own
different intellectual activities. One is conscious of the difference between the two cognitive acts and, accordingly, of the
difference in their objects. But whether the difference between
the objects implies that these are really different in the thing
itself, is as yet not at all clear.

"Man" and "animal" are different objects of consideration,
but there is no real difference between them in the thing in
which they are found. For all that the reasoning so far has
concluded, the case may be the same in regard to a thing and
its existence.[21] The distinction set up between them may be
only the work of human reason. However, a distinction
effected by human reason may be based upon aspects in the
thing that in point of fact require real distinction from each
other. Distinction through human reason does not necessarily exclude distinction in reality. But whether or not there
is real distinction in the present case is not immediately apparent, and has to be left for later consideration.[22]

These characteristics of existence enable one to deal with
a number of the questions concerning it. How is one able to
speak about it, to make it a subject for investigation and study?
The answer is apparent from what has just been considered.
Existence is conceptualized as a subject in itself, and in this

---

[21] Cf.: ". . . here an accident means what does not belong to the notion
of something, as 'rational' is called accidental to 'animal'; and in this way
being is accidental to every created quiddity, because it does not belong to
the notion of the quiddity itself." St. Thomas, *In I Sententiarum*, d. 8,
expos. lae partis textus; I, 209.

[22] See Chapter V, nn. 6 ff.; Chapter VI, nn. 10–11.

guise is given cognitional existence in the mind just as anything else that is being discussed. But unlike other subjects of discussion, the existence of things did not offer any aspect that could at once be grasped through conceptualization. It had to be known first through judgment. What was attained through judgment was then represented as something, as an actuality of perfection, as a synthesis, or as an attribute or predicate.

All these notions are universal, and represent in universal fashion the highly individual synthesizing grasped through judgment. These notions, moreover, are all taken from the realms that form the object of conceptualization. They make manifest the aspects to which things and natures give rise. They cannot contain in authentic fashion anything that is characteristically existential. The best they can do is to draw attention to and focus attention upon what is originally known through a judgment. Spotlighting the object so known, they can allow existential conclusions to be drawn from it. Because they are universal, they permit syllogistic reasoning. Because they base the reasoning on what is known through judgment, they can lead to an existential conclusion. But if their focus is removed for a moment from what the judgment is grasping and they are taken just in themselves, they have no ability whatever to provide a ground that would allow one to reason to any existence or to any nonexistence.

The notorious ontological argument for the existence of God is perhaps the most outstanding attempt at this kind of reasoning.[23] In it, in one way or another, one takes one's

---

[23] A collection of the outstanding views on the ontological argument may be found in *The Ontological Argument*, ed. Alvin Plantinga (Garden City, New York: Doubleday, 1965). Unfortunately the interesting mediaeval developments given the Anselmian argument by Bonaventure and Duns Scotus are not included. There is considerable doubt, moreover, in regard to the propriety of calling the arguments of Anselm or of Bonaventure "ontological." The sources of the ontological reasoning in Duns Scotus have not yet been sufficiently explored. Accordingly, the historical origin and background of the ontological argument can hardly claim at the present moment to be adequately understood.

concept of perfection and extends it without limit. It is thereby
made to possess all perfections, including real existence. Accordingly, it is shown to be knowledge of an object that really
exists, on the claims of this argument. But the concept of
perfection, as the preceding considerations have made clear, is
taken from the realm of the categories. No matter how much
it is expanded, even to the infinite, it does not get outside that
order. It never gets into the realm of existence. What it
embraces is solely what is grasped through conceptualization,
and not what is grasped through judgment. To conclude to
existence, it would have to reach outside the range of objects
attained through conceptualization and focus upon existence
grasped through judgment. But it is this very existence of the
most perfect object that is in question. The existence has to
be proven in the conclusion, according to the structure of the
argument, and therefore cannot be granted in the premises.

For the same reason any inversions of the ontological argument in the direction of nonexistence turn out to be invalid.
It has been claimed that an agnostic attitude toward God
involves an outright denial of his existence, since "God must
be 'One Whose existence . . . we cannot possibly conceive
away.' "[24] The possibility of denying God's existence entails,
accordingly, his "necessary non-existence."

This way of reasoning fails in the same way as the regular
ontological argument. In themselves, concepts just do not reach
the existential order. They tell nothing about the existence
or nonexistence of their objects. True, a concept that combined contradictories would thereby preclude the real existence
of its object, for instance, the concept of a square circle or
of a stick with only one end. In the present case, however,
contradictory characteristics of this type are not involved. No
matter how adequate an object of worship may be conceived,

---

[24] J. N. Findlay, "Can God's Existence be Disproved?" *Mind*, LVII
(1948), 182.

the conceptualization just in itself cannot entail that the object exists. Knowledge of its existence would have to come from a different source, from what is known through judgment. Neither its real existence, nor its nonexistence in reality, contradicts anything contained in its conceptualization, when existence is meant to convey the notion that it does exist. It is quite possible to doubt that the most perfect object exists in reality, without admitting that its nonexistence follows necessarily from the content in its concept.

There is also an objection to the notion of cognitional existence that may be classed as an inversion of the ontological argument. It has been objected that cognitional existence allows "nonexistence" to receive existence in the mind, with the resultant paradox that nonexistence exists. This paradox need cause little trouble, for what has taken place is clear enough. In making "nonexistence" a subject for discussion, one takes existence as the object of a concept and, accordingly, as a subject set up in its own right, negates it with a tilde, and in this way arrives at "nonexistence" as a subject for consideration and inquiry. There is no more difficulty here than in the concept of a square circle. The consequence is that nonexistence does exist as an object in the mind. But the paradox is only apparent, and vanishes when one reflects on the different roles of conceptualization and judgment.

Like any other concept, the concept of nonexistence does not entail that its object exists or that it does not exist. It gives no information on that score. Nothing in its content, therefore, can be contradictory to the fact that it exists. Through reflective judgment one knows as a fact that it does exist in one's mind while one is thinking about it. But it exhibits no nature that would be capable of existing in reality, any more than does a square circle.

The study of these characteristics of existence likewise shows how existence can appear to some thinkers as an entirely

empty concept, and to others as the richest and most meaningful of all objects. The whole conceptual content in the notion
of existence is taken from nonexistential sources, from the
categories. If no other origin than the conceptual is allowed
for knowable content, the concept of existence will necessarily
appear empty. If a different source is recognized for knowledge
of existence, namely judgment, the concept, though itself nonexistential in content, may be the means of focusing upon the
content known through judgment and using it in universalized
fashion for reasoning processes.

Similarly, the questions whether existence is a predicate or
a perfection receive different answers as they are approached
from these different ways of knowing existence. If conceptualization alone is recognized as the means of knowing existence,
no characteristically new notion or perfection is found for
predication. What is known through judgment, on the other
hand, gives something very meaningful to be predicated of the
thing and able to enrich it with vistas that open out into a
realm beyond the observable world of finite natures.

Finally, the way in which existence is conceptualized shows
how one can conceive something as really existent without
meaning that it does really exist. When Napoleon in Browning's poem projected the taking of Ratisbon, he was thinking
of its capture in actual reality, not just an imaginary capture.
Yet the conceiving of the real capture as taking place in real
existence was not enough to assure him that it actually would
take place:

> My plans
> That soar, to earth may fall,
> Let once my army-leader Lannes
> Waver at yonder wall
> ("Incident of the French Camp").

The concept "real existence" is in itself formed from notions taken from the order of the categories. Just in itself

it has no other content. The content of the concept "existence" is that of "something," "perfection," or "actuality" — all originally categorical notions. The content of "real" is taken from the notion of thing. Combining the two does not place the composite concept outside the realm attained by conceptualization. It does not tell one whether anything does exist. This explains how one can conceive a mountain of gold as really existent in the Himalayas without being compelled to think that it does exist there; indeed, he can conceive this even when he believes that it does not exist there.

The characteristics manifested by existence, then, offer abundant help for answering questions about it. They also lead to further inquiry. The radically incomplete and accidental status of the existence known in observable things seems to open up on something outside itself. Besides manifesting its own intrinsic characteristics, accordingly, does the existence of things lead the mind to anything extrinsic to itself? That is the next question that suggests itself for investigation. But in approaching the question, one has to keep constantly in mind the salient points that have emerged from the foregoing study of the way existence is conceptualized. In any reasoning from the existence of things, existence has to be represented in the universal concepts just considered. In this way all things are brought under the general notion of existents; middle terms are available for reasoning, and commonly shared notions of existence permit verbal communication. To have the reasoning based on the characteristic content of existence, however, the universal concepts have to keep spotlighting what is grasped through judgment. A portrait continues to reveal the features of an opera singer in her absence, but the spotlight ceases to show them once it has been flashed off her actual presence on the stage.

An authentic concept of existence would by itself carry the message that something exists. As the case actually is, on the contrary, any of our reasoning in the order of existence has to be based continually upon existence that is being known through judgment. "The existence of whooping cranes" is indeed a convenient and indispensable way of referring to the fact that whooping cranes exist. But unless it is spotlighting what is known in the judgment that they do exist, this concept of existence is not capable of offering any genuinely existential information. Just in itself, like "the existence of flying saucers," it is open to either affirmation or negation. The concept does not give the information that its object exists or does not exist. Unless the concept focuses attention on existence as known through a different activity, it will as in the ontological argument fail to ground any existential conclusions. We have no authentic concept of existence. What we do is use concepts of other objects to indicate actual existence and to keep attention concentrated upon it. But no concept taken just in itself expresses what is characteristic of the fact that something exists.

The concept of existence, in a word, is not exactly a hyaline. Its content is the content of some other concept, whether of "something," of "actuality," of "perfection," or of a "synthesis." Each of these has its own pigments, but none of them tinctures existence. Rather, the observable character of existence lies in the object that is being known through judgment, and upon which the concept merely focuses one's intellectual gaze. Authentic knowledge of existence does not originate in any concept, no matter how well it is tinctured. There need be little surprise that the characteristic role of existence escaped the ancient Greek thinkers, that it was bracketed by Husserl's phenomenology as irrelevant to scientific consideration, and that it has led modern writers to brand the concept as empty or diaphanous.

A further point is just as important for the ensuing investigation as the one just considered. Not only do the characteristics of existence have to be kept steadily in mind, but they also should be given the full play of their bearing upon one another. They are not to be viewed in isolation. The one has to equalize the other's impact. The accidental character of existence, as has been noted,[25] has to be balanced by the necessary function that existence exercises in the thing. A corresponding caution is in order when existence is said to lie outside the nature because it is not part of the thing's nature. This again is true, but has to be balanced by a complementary tenet. As the most basic actuality of the thing, existence is most intimate. It is the most inward of all the thing's characteristics. It is the core of all else, the axis around which all the rest revolves, even though it is not part of the thing's nature. From within, however, it is actuating everything in the nature. It has both features, and it has them by exercising the one role of existence. It could not be the existence of something other than itself unless at the same time it both lay outside the thing's nature and actuated the nature most intimately from within. Both features are imperative. The one complements the other.

Similar therapy has to be applied in regarding existence as something that is other than the thing's nature. Here one is obviously conceptualizing the thing's existence as a separate object for consideration, and contrasting it with the thing's nature as with another object. The process is perfectly legitimate, as has been seen,[26] and is a requirement for the philosophical treatment of the two. Each is represented separately as though it were a distinct reality in itself, in the manner in which any object is conceptualized to serve as a subject of predication and inquiry. For the ensuing study, then, each of them has to be represented as though it were independently constituted in itself. In this cognitional distinction of the one

---

25 Cf. n. 19 of this chapter.
26 Cf. n. 1 of this chapter.

from the other, they can be thought of as distinct objects
attained by two different mental activities, with existence as
accidental to the thing's nature, prior to the nature, essential
to the nature, outside the nature, and most intimate to the
nature. The two objects are considered as related to each other
in all these ways. But not for a moment should this conceptual manner of representing existence be allowed to give
the impression that the existence is a reality in itself or that
it in any manner plays the role of subject in the way it is
exercised. There is but the one reality involved, and that is
the existent thing.

CHAPTER IV

Cause of Existence

The characteristics exhibited by existence, when examined separately, have proven rich in content and in interest. They show clearly that existence is far from a blank or empty or meaningless object. They break out in multiple facets that lure the intellect to deeper penetration of their import. At first sight they are filled with oddities, oddities that would lead to despair if existence had to be assessed as originally the object of a concept, but that level off into promising vistas when existence is understood to be grasped originally through judgment and only subsequently conceptualized.

Taken separately, then, the characteristics of existence vie in interest with those of other leading philosophical objects. But what happens when they are considered in conjunction, one with another? Does any cross-fertilization take place toward new and otherwise unachievable philosophic strains? Does the impregnation initiate a reasoning process that will result in important and distinctive conclusions? Does the combined impact of the various characteristics engender philosophic progeny peculiarly its own? Does it give birth to authentic metaphysical knowledge that might justify the claim of existence to hold in its meaning the spiritual destiny of the West?

Take, for a starting point, the accidental feature in an observable thing's existence. At first sight it may not appear to be of too much significance. Most obviously it is expressed in the consideration that the thing may lose existence, just as it may lose a certain degree of size or weight, or a certain color. A man may lose hair, teeth, and health and, finally, bodily existence. In this perspective the accidental character of existence does not seem to offer any special problem or challenge. Even in contexts in the past in which existence was not regarded as capable of being lost, its accidental character did not on this account present any extraordinary difficulty.

Against an Aristotelian background a medieval thinker could hold that the observable heavenly bodies were indestructible, and yet consider their existence as accidental to them on the ground that it was not contained within their natures. Against a Christian background, for the same reason, angels and spiritual souls may be regarded as indestructible even though existence is considered as accidental to them. These cases, at least from the immediate viewpoint of accidental character, do not bring out anything anomalous in the role played by existence. The notion of an inseparable accident is quite traditional. The regular example was man's ability to laugh. Intellect and will, at least in any setting in which they are regarded as belonging to the second division of the Aristotelian category of quality, are readily recognized instances of accidents that are really inseparable from human nature.

No, the peculiar challenge here does not arise from either the separable or inseparable role of existence as an accident. It comes from another and altogether distinctive source. One may speak of a man losing hair, teeth, and health. He is still a man, the subject who did the losing and who though bedridden can still go on losing, be it only his patience. A blonde can change color after color in her hair, and still remain the same person who undergoes the alterations in appearance. But is the sense even remotely the same when you say a thing acquires or loses existence? A subject was there to acquire the new color or to lose the hair and teeth. But what subject was there to acquire or to lose existence? Is the meaning at all the same? Without existence, how could the subject be there to acquire or to lose anything? When you speak of a table acquiring existence, surely the meaning is different from its acquiring a new color. As an existent, the table already was there to become white, or red, or brown, or any other color you care to paint it. But in acquiring existence, the table was not already there to acquire this accidental perfection. There was wood, already existent. But you are not saying that the wood begins to exist. You say, and mean, that the table begins to exist as the cabinetmaker proceeds with his work. The wood acquires an accidental perfection in the fourth division of the Aristotelian category of quality. It becomes an artifact. But it is the artifact, not the wood, that has now begun to exist. The consideration stands out all the more clearly in the case of a plant or an animal. The plant or the animal obviously was not there to acquire its own existence in the same sense as it acquires new coloring or greater size.

Similarly, though perhaps not quite so obviously, is the sense different in the case of losing existence. A subject is there to lose weight or color or size. It is there to do the losing. But to the extent to which the subject is losing existence, can it be spoken of as there to do the losing? Without existence, it is nothing. It is not there to do any losing, even the losing of existence. The losing of existence automatically removes the subject for the losing, even in the attempt to represent it as there to undergo the loss. Delusion is very easy here. One is accustomed to regard a subject as losing its attributes and possessions once they cease to be present for it. Why not regard existence in the same way when it ceases to actuate the subject? The difference between the two cases, however, should be clear enough upon reflection. In the one case the subject could be there without the attribute in question, and accordingly could be conceived as losing it. But without existence, there is just no subject there to be conceived as having or as losing anything. The notion of a subject losing existence negates itself, if it is understood in the same way as losing other perfections. The existence that is being lost is presupposed as still present in constituting the subject that is losing it.

Yet it makes excellent sense to say that a table or a plant or an animal loses existence. No matter what circumlocutions are used, as in saying "It ceases to exist," the way of representation remains parallel. The artifact or plant or animal is set up in cognitional existence as a subject of a proposition, and the predicate of real existence is separated from it. The procedure is thoroughly legitimate, as in the case of any predication of existence. What justifies, then, the discrepancy of meaning between the case of a subject losing a color or a configuration, and the case of a subject losing existence?

The presupposition of existence for a subject that is acquiring or losing anything, even existence itself, immediately brings in one of the other characteristics of existence. This is the priority of existence to the thing it actuates. Although existence is an accidental perfection of the thing, it does not follow upon the thing as do the predicamental accidents. Rather, it precedes the thing; it is prior to the thing. Unless the existence is presupposed, the thing would not be there at all. Existence may be an accident, but it has to be an accident that is prior to the thing itself, prior to its substance, prior to its nature. The priority, of course, is a priority of metaphysical order, and in no way a priority of time.

What consequences does this combination of prior and accidental status have for the interpretation of existence? At once the question of dependence arises. An accident in its very notion involves dependence. It is a perfection' of something else; it is inherent *in* something else. In explaining the notion of inherence in or presence in a subject, Aristotle described the accidental perfection as "being incapable of existence apart from the said subject."[1] It is not something there in its own right. It requires something else to permit it to have being. It is *of* or *in* something else in the sense of being dependent upon a subject in its very notion. A color, in its very notion, has to qualify a surface. Without a surface, the color would be inconceivable. A size has to be the size of a body. Without the notion of body, "size" would not even make sense. In general, an accident has been understood traditionally as a being of a being. In this manner it has to be dependent upon another being. If it were not dependent upon something else, it would be there in its own self, in its own right. It would be a substance, not an accident.

Is there any way of eliminating this aspect of dependence in the notion of an accident? Can it be done without self-contradiction? What would an accident signify if the note of dependence were deleted from its concept? It would be a thing by itself, in the sense that iron or a maple tree or an elephant is a thing just in itself. The requirement that it is something *of* something else would disappear. Gone also would be the notion that it is *in* something else, in the sense in which Aristotle required it to be in a subject. You would have a color, for instance, that was not the color of anything, a color that was not found on any surface, just as a tree is not the tree of anything nor is it in this sense found in any subject. The note of dependence, accordingly, cannot disappear from the notion of an accident without completely destroying the

---

[1] *Categories*, 2,1a25; Oxford tr.

accident. The very presence of an accident involves its dependence on something else.

Where the accident is existence, what is the "something
else" upon which it is dependent? Certainly the accident is the
existence of the thing in which it inheres, say of the table or
the plant or the animal. From that viewpoint it would call for
dependence upon the nature and individual it actuates. Unless
it is the existence of a stone or a tree or a man or of something else in the observable world, existence as we immediately
know it in judgment could not be found. It has to be the
existence of a thing.[2] Similarly, it is always found in the thing
— the metal, the plant, the animal, or in whatever else exists
in the observable universe. It is never found in itself, but only
in the thing it is actuating.

In these two respects, then, existence conforms closely
enough to the status of predicamental accidents. But what
about the crucial consideration that, unlike all predicamental
accidents, it is prior to the subject it is actuating? Where a
subject is already existent, it is quite easy to conceive the
accident as being of the subject and in the subject. As a visual
aid one can conjure up the image of the accident being in
the subject somewhat as a coat of paint is on the outside
surfaces of a car, and is clung to tenaciously as a possession
wherever the car goes as it rolls up its thousands in mileage.
In this way an accident readily can be imagined (though far
from correctly) as being in and of its subject. But where the
subject cannot be conceived as already there to receive the
accident, the imagery breaks down completely.

With existence one has the anomaly of an accident that is,
indeed, in and of its subject, but which has to be presup-

---

[2] Cf.: "If, then, being is not in a subject, there will remain no way in
which that which is other than being can be united to it. Now, being, as
being, cannot be diverse; but it can be diversified by something beside itself;
thus, the being of a stone is other than that of a man." St. Thomas, *Summa
Contra Gentiles*, II, 52, Si enim; tr. James F. Anderson under the title *On
the Truth of the Catholic Faith*, Vol. II (New York: Doubleday Image,
1956), p. 153.

posed before one can have the subject. To have any actuality at all, the subject has to presuppose its own existence. In this respect the subject is dependent upon the existence, and not vice versa. To have any accident at all as in it and of it, the subject has to have its own actuality. Even to have its own existence in it and of it, the subject must presuppose its own actualization through existence. It cannot be viewed as first being there to receive existence and to be characterized by existence. Rather, before there can be question of any function of the subject at all, does it not have to be regarded as existing?

This means, obviously enough, that on account of its priority there is an important sense in which existence is not dependent upon the subject it actuates. From the viewpoint of existence itself, may not this priority be called the most important sense of the notion? It is what radically distinguishes existence from all other accidents in the thing, and gives it its characteristic role as existence. No other accident is required in order to give the subject the status of something in itself. No other consideration could allow existence to qualify as the actuality of all actualities and the perfection of all perfections. The priority to all else is the distinctive characteristic of existence when it is conceptualized as actuality.

In its most important and distinctive sense, then, existence is not dependent upon the subject it actuates. In this it differs radically from all other accidents. Can it therefore be regarded as independent in its fundamental priority to its subject? Hardly. That would be to give it the status of something in itself. It would make existence a substance. If the existence were independent in its priority to the substance it actuates, it would be there in itself regardless of subsequent specification. It would no longer be an accident. To the full extent to which it is accidental — and that includes its whole notion — the existence of observable things has to be dependent, dependent upon something else.

But upon what? Certainly not just upon the thing it actuates; this has become apparent from its prior status in regard to its subject. If in this respect of priority it is dependent upon something, it is certainly dependent on something other than the subject in which it inheres.

The import and the unusual direction of this reasoning would be hard to overemphasize. Here one is dealing with a characteristic in the existent thing that leads to something in no way already contained within the formal notion of the thing or in its existence. The process cannot at all be described as "unpacking" what was hidden away within. It is a journeying to something not contained within the original data. The reasoning fails to determine what the thing thereby reached is. That it does exist, however, insofar as it is something upon which the existence investigated depends, is cogently implied. If it did not itself exist, it would not be there to function as the "something else" upon which the existence in question is dependent. The conclusion, accordingly, is not something about the thing with which one started. It does not consist in making explicit any feature that was already contained in implicit fashion within the thing. It is not at all a reiteration of the assertion that the thing is dependent upon something else. That was one of the premises. Rather, it is a conclusion about the "something else." It is the conclusion that the "something else" exists.

Is not this a different kind of reasoning from any in logic or in mathematics? In the procedure of these disciplines, what is implicit in the premises is made explicit in the conclusions. Hence logic and mathematics could appear to logical positivism as tautological procedures. Hence also they could be regarded as "unpacking" data that had been stored inside the premises. But even here is the description any too accurate? Were the conclusions in fact contained within either premise taken separately? Were they not, rather, born of the conjunction of the premises in the vital activity of thinking? Is not the process creative of new knowledge, and not an unearthing of the old?

The conclusion that the angles of a triangle are equal to two right angles is not contained in the definition of a triangle. Nor is it contained in the notion of a parallel line drawn through the apex. But these two notions when taken together result in the new knowledge contained in the conclusion. Both logic and mathematics, accordingly, may be regarded as creative in their activity. Yet what they reason to remains somehow within the ambit marked off by the combined premises. It stays within the limits of formal sequence from the two. Though the conclusion is new, the entities involved remain the same. The equality of the angles to two right angles does not get away from the triangle itself. But the "something else" to which the reasoning from existence leads does not at all follow in formal sequence from the thing's nature nor from the content of its existence. It is something that gets away from the thing itself and its existence, something that is thoroughly outside both.

Yet when the premises are brought together they engender the new conclusion that some other thing exists, that there is something upon which the observable thing is dependent for its existence. Upon what type of sequence is the reasoning based? Have we any firsthand experience of a type of sequence different from that of the formal sequence of one notion from another?

We do in fact have immediate knowledge of one quite obvious area in which the sequence is other than formal. Are we not conscious of the way in which our thoughts and free decisions issue from ourselves? The sequence is not formal. It is not the type of sequence by which conclusions follow from premises in geometry. Rather, it is a type of sequence by which thoughts and decisions that did not exist before are brought into being. We produce them; we bring them into existence. The traditional term for this type of causality goes back to the Aristotelian commentators. It is called efficient causality.[3]

There is no possibility of reasoning to the notion of efficient causality. It is already too late for that. By the very effort made in initiating the reasoning process, one would be in immediate possession of the notion. It would be too late to try to acquire it as a conclusion. It is known, accordingly, through immediate experience. It is already grasped as one pursues any course of reasoning, including any attempted reasoning to the notion itself. One knows immediately, therefore, the meaning of causality that gives existence to something new. The problem lies elsewhere.

The problem is to know whether this type of sequence is required for the existence of observable things that we grasp through judgment, but without experience of the causality by which their existence might be produced. Through judgment we know the real existence of sensible things directly. But we have no direct awareness of any causality that produces them. We are aware of the succession of events, but not of the causal sequence. We see the movement and contact of match with stone, and then we see the flame. But we do not see or in any way experience the causing of the one by the other.[4] We

---

[3] "Efficient" has here the sense of making or producing or doing. An efficient cause is a cause that makes or does something. The obsolete English "factive" would translate the Greek word more exactly. Regardless of terminology, however, the notion of an efficient cause is too compelling to be banished permanently from philosophical consideration. Cf.: "This ancient idea of an efficient cause . . . is generally considered by contemporary philosophers to be metaphysical and obscure, and quite plainly erroneous. . . . I believe, on the contrary, that while this older metaphysical idea of an efficient cause is not an easy one to grasp, it is nonetheless superior and far closer to the truth of things than the conceptions of causation that are now usually taken for granted." Richard Taylor, "Causation," The Monist, XLVII (1963), p. 291.

[4] See Malebranche, Entretiens sur la Métaphysique, VII, 10; Hume, A Treatise of Human Nature, I,3,3; Josef Geyser, Das Prinzip vom zureichenden Grunde (Regensburg, 1929), pp. 52–57.

have no immediate knowledge of efficient causality in anything other than our own internal activity.

The problem, then, is whether the existence of each thing in the observable world is produced by something else. While it is too late to base one's original awareness of efficient causality on anything other than immediate experience, there remains nevertheless the question of applying the notion to things other than one's own internal activity. But is not that exactly what the reasoning just undertaken demands? Wherever a thing's existence is accidental to its nature, the existence, because it is prior to the thing's nature, is dependent upon something other than the thing itself. Through experience of internal activity one knows what dependence for existence is. It is dependence upon an efficient cause. There is no basis for projecting one's own type of efficient causality on anything else. But that there is such a process as efficient causality, is known immediately. That the process is different from formal sequence also is clearly recognizable. From immediate experience, too, one knows that the process consists in an activity different from its product, and that the activity itself is really existent during the producing.

In that setting one is able to understand what kind of dependence is involved by an existence accidental to a nature. It is dependence upon a real activity that is other than the thing produced, and other than any of the accidents that follow upon the thing's nature. The accidental and prior character of the existence grasped through judgment, even though as yet one does not know whether that existence is really or only conceptually distinct from the thing, provides the basis for proof that it is being caused efficiently by something else.

Does this reasoning show whether the activity that produces the existence is itself an agent, or merely the accident of an agent different from itself? The reasoning seems to give no immediate information about the particular nature of the efficient cause. It proves only that there is an efficient cause at work, and that the existence is from the start as well as afterwards dependent upon the causal activity. But it gives no immediate insight into the cause's nature. The activity of a cause other than one's self is in no way experienced. It can only be reasoned to. Nor does the reasoning so far reveal whether the same efficient cause that first produces the thing continues to be the cause upon which the thing's existence depends. As far as the argument goes, could not another cause be substituted at any moment for the continuance of activity sufficient to keep effecting the existence? Is there anything in the reasoning that requires the unicity of the efficient cause? Rather, are not the exigencies of the argument satisfied as long as there is some activity at work upon which the existence of the observable thing may continue to depend?

Furthermore, the existence of the activity or agent also could be accidental. The reasoning so far has nothing to say on that point. But if the existence were accidental, would it not, for the reasons just considered, be dependent, correspondingly, upon some other efficient causality? Would it too not be dependent upon something other than the nature it is actuating? The reasoning applies just as cogently in its case as in the case of the observable thing from which the demonstration started. Must one thereby open an infinite regress of efficient causes? Or could one represent them as causing each other's existence in circular fashion? But in either case would not the sum total of these causes be a collection of natures none of which originated existence? If such series of causes are projected on reality as the sum total of things, do they not involve the conclusion that absolutely nothing exists in the universe? None of the things individually would of itself be a source of existential actuality. How then could their sum total be in any way a source for it? How would any existence whatsoever be introduced into the world? There would be no means at all for having anything exist. Whether projected as infinite in number or as circular in causality, each thing whose existence is accidental to its nature would be in itself existentially a zero. Their sum total also would be zero from the standpoint of existential content.

Yet each thing in these series is projected as factually having existence. Each is regarded as an active efficient cause, actively producing existence. But the existence in each case is dependent existence. The sum total, consequently, remains dependent existence. All the existence present in these causes, accordingly, will be dependent on something other than the sum total of the things projected as so existing. All the existence is therefore being caused by something outside the totality. Any existence that is accidental to a nature ultimately has to be caused by an activity whose existence is not accidental to its nature nor prior to its nature, but, on the contrary, coincident with its nature. It has to be caused efficiently by an activity whose very nature is existence.

What will this mean? Will it not mean at least that the activity exists in itself, since its nature is existence? It will be at once activity and substance. Activity and agent will coincide, and both will coincide with existence. In a word, existence here is the nature, the substance. It is *what* exists. In traditional terminology it has been called subsistent existence.[5] The expression means that here existence subsists in itself, is found in itself and not in something else, in contrast to existence that is an accident. In this case existence itself is the substance.

---

[5] "Subsist," though meaning in the original Latin to stand still or to halt, has in this traditional use the overtones of "substance." It means to exist as a substance. This is quite different from Chisholm's use of "subsist" to translate Meinong's *bestehen*, as applied to an object that is knowable but does not by any means exist; see *Realism and the Background of Phenomenology*, ed. Roderick M. Chisholm (Glencoe, Ill.: The Free Press, 1960), p. 79.

Of this kind of existence we have of course no immediate experience. As in the case of any other efficient causality outside ourselves, we know it only in the conclusion of a demonstration. We know thereby that it exists. But unlike other efficient causes, causes whose nature is not existence, it does not seem to present any nature that could be conceptualized. If its very nature is existence, how can we conceptualize it? We have no authentic concept of existence. Nothing in the concepts we do form of existence has anything characteristically existential in its content. How, then, can we have even the basis for developing a concept of subsistent existence? Have we here any relevant conceptual ground upon which to work? Have we any basic conceptual content at all to elaborate? Mystics may report experimental knowledge of some kind, but in respect of its own typical content the knowledge in every case turns out to be incommunicable. From the standpoint of conceptual knowledge, which is communicable, must not subsistent existence remain entirely unknown, utterly unknown, to the human mind?[6]

Christian tradition, especially in the Neoplatonic cast, has made much of this entirely negative character of genuine theological knowledge. Against that background the sharp contrast between metaphysical knowledge and the knowledge afforded by the experimental sciences becomes intensified. As already noted, reasoning in the order of existence is different from the reasoning processes in logic and in mathematics. In these sciences the reasoning follows the lines of formal causality. With existence, it is based upon the sequence of efficient causality. In the experimental sciences, outside problems of formal classification, the search is as a rule for efficient

---

[6] The expressions of St. Thomas in this regard are "omnino ignotum" ("entirely unknown") (*In Epistolam ad Romanos*, I, 6; ed. Vivès, XX, 398b) and "penitus . . . ignotum" ("utterly unknown") (*Summa Contra Gentiles*, III, 49, Cognoscit). On the topic, see Anton C. Pegis, "Penitus Manet Ignotum," *Mediaeval Studies*, XXVII (1965), pp. 212–226.

causes. One is seeking to find the particles that cause the various pointer readings, the viruses that cause the common cold, the atmospheric disturbances that cause hurricanes. In every case in this sphere one can work out a concept of the cause that is being sought, form hypotheses about its nature and activity, and then observe and experiment to check one's theories.

If experience verifies the theories, the causes conjectured hypothetically are accepted as proven, often with the hope that further scientific progress will bring them under direct observation. So the presence of molecules was established as the cause for certain observable phenomena. Only much later did molecules themselves become visible through the electron microscope. Atoms, on the contrary, have not yet become visible, though a new microscope now promises that they soon will come under human vision. But in all these cases the nature of the causes is in principle conceivable. If this nature explains the observable phenomena to the scientist's satisfaction, as verified by experiment and tabulation, the existence of the cause is accepted as established. A continued record of subsequent finding of causes already theoretically established justifies the confidence placed in this method.

From a metaphysical viewpoint there is, of course, in this procedure no strict demonstration of existence. The existence of the particular cause is at first conjectured, then developed into a hypothesis, and finally accepted when the hypothesis is verified. A method of this kind is not open to metaphysics. In showing that all existence that is accidental has to be caused by something else, metaphysics has neither the means nor the need of first conjecturing the particular nature of the cause. It merely establishes the existence of some cause, regardless of what the nature of the cause may be. It has no means of verifying this conclusion by further observation or experiment. The causal sequence itself is not observable except in the case of one's own internal activities, and no means are available for bringing things into existence experimentally in clear-cut exclusion of efficient causality.

The metaphysician can check his conclusions only by scrutinizing carefully each step of his reasoning. He has not at his disposal the ready double check of verification. But on the level of existence he does demonstrate that wherever existence is accidental, it is being caused efficiently by something other than the thing it makes exist. In a context of probable reasoning Plato[7] had formulated the principle that whatever comes into being is produced by a cause. Descartes[8] maintained that independently of things the mind has the knowledge of the eternal truths. Among these he mentioned, in tautological form, that whatever is made cannot escape the condition of being made. Against this background the notion of a universal "principle of causality" was developed and attacked.[9] It could allow the experimental scientist to hold as granted that anything taking place had to have something to cause it, and that the only problem was to find out what that something is. In a context where knowledge of the *kind* of things and activities alone really mattered, the "principle of causality" became used to justify the uniform application of scientific findings. It became "same cause, same effect," instead of "every event has an efficient cause." Readmitted into the domain of philosophy under this new meaning, it gave rise to the astonishing conclusion that freedom is incompatible with causality.

These considerations emphasize strongly the difference of metaphysical reasoning from the procedure of the experimental sciences as well as from that of logic and of mathematics. Unlike these other sciences, metaphysical reasoning is not

---

[7] *Timaeus*, 28AC; *Philebus*, 26E.

[8] *Principia Philosophiae*, I, 49.

[9] Further discussion of this topic may be found in my articles, "The Causal Proposition — Principle or Conclusion?" *The Modern Schoolman*, XXXII (1955), pp. 159–171; 257–270; 323–339, and "The Causal Proposition Revisited," *ibid.*, XLIV (1967), 143–151.

based upon natures or essences or kinds of things. Its starting point is the existence of these things, and it progresses in an order different from that of essence. But what happens when it faces an existence that at the same time is an essence? This is the case now under scrutiny. Metaphysics has no characteristic basis in the nature of anything to reason to that other nature. It will have to remain based upon the existential aspect. Yet here it has no authentic concept to serve as a runway for a flight to the higher level. Must its knowledge of subsistent being remain, then, entirely negative? Or does the existential basis afford the means of attaining truly positive knowledge in this regard?

Without any authentic or characteristic concept of existence, one cannot hope to know *what* existence is, even in an incipient way. All one can know is *that* things exist. Where the thing in question is subsistent existence, one can likewise know merely that it exists, in the conclusion of the reasoning process just undertaken. You may say that one thereby knows that it is a substance, and at least to that extent knows what it is. True, but *what* substance means on the level on which it is identical with existence, one does not know any more than one knows what existence itself is. One knows that it is an activity, but again, what activity means when its nature is existence, one does not know at all. One knows similarly that subsistent existence has all the transcendental properties, for these properties follow necessarily upon existence. Subsistent existence is one, true, good, beautiful. But one just does not know *what* unity, truth, goodness, and beauty mean on the level of this kind of existence.

Furthermore, one knows that existence is the actuality of all actualities. Where it subsists in itself, then, will it not be actualizing within itself every other perfection whatsoever? It is the actuality of them all, and when it is the nature that subsists it is their actual presence. It is therefore the subsistent unity and sum total of all perfections. Accordingly, every accomplishment, every virtue, every activity, is found within subsistent existence to the full extent to which each is a perfection. Knowledge, love, wisdom, justice, mercy, power, and the like, are all present in subsistent existence insofar as they have the aspect of perfection.

May we not conclude, consequently, *that* every perfection whatsoever, no matter where we encounter it in the universe, is also contained within subsistent existence? But *what* any of them means when found in thoroughgoing identity with subsistent existence, we do not know at all. Each of them is subsistent existence,[10] and what subsistent existence is cannot be conceived on the basis of the data from which we reason. We can know them only as identical with existence, and of existence we have no authentic or characteristic concept. Yet does not the fact of knowing that subsistent existence contains in itself all actual and possible perfections make our knowledge of it extremely rich? Has it not enabled Christian thinkers to develop the whole positive theology about subsistent being? Is it not sufficient to launch the human mind into a veritable ocean of intelligibility?[11] Where a perfection involves no essential imperfection in its own notion, as in the case of knowledge or of free choice, it may be predicated here in its own full sense, even though the notion escapes our conceptual grasp when the perfection is identified with subsistent existence. We know for certain that it is contained within subsistent existence, and that is sufficient to allow the predication to be made. Accordingly, we may conclude that subsistent existence is intelligent, wise, just, and free. There is nothing symbolic or metaphorical in this predication.

---

[10] See St. Thomas, *De Veritate*, II, 11c; *De Potentia*, VII, 5c.

[11] The metaphor of "an infinite and unlimited sea of being (ousias)" is used to express this nature in Gregory Nazianzen, *Oratio XXXVIII*, 7, 9 (Migne's *Patrologia Graeca*, XXXVI, 317B), and John Damascene, *De Fide Orth.*, I, 9, 30 (Migne's *Patrologia Graeca*, XCIV, 836B).

The notions are meant in their literal sense, with the clear understanding that the instances of these perfections in the world around us are only secondary. Their primary instance is to be found in subsistent being. But both primary and secondary instances exhibit the perfection in its exact literal sense.

On the other hand, activities and qualifications such as walking, anger, jealousy, solidity, hearing, sight, and the like, are indeed perfections or actualities, but with a mixture of imperfection in their very notions. The perfection in these objects is duly actualized by existence, just as is the perfection in any other object. Where existence subsists, it will, as their actuality, necessarily contain all their perfection. But it cannot contain them as they are expressed by their own characteristic notions, that is, in their literal sense. As limited by material restrictions, these notions involve imperfection and are inseparable from imperfection. In their literal sense, therefore, they cannot be identical with subsistent being, which, as the subsistent perfection of all perfections allows no room for any imperfection. Any imperfection at all would restrict its scope and prevent it from subsisting as the perfection of all perfections. But sight and hearing require material and limited organs; anger and jealousy are emotions of a material nature. When applied to subsistent being, predicates like these signify a corresponding though radically different perfection, by way of analogy in metaphor or symbolism. Sight and intelligence, for instance, are radically different cognitive activities, yet both give cognition in analogous ways. Sight, accordingly, may be used metaphorically for intelligence. The perfection in the cognitional activity is retained. The imperfection, namely the organic requirement and restriction, disappears.

In this way the marvelously rich symbolism of the Scriptures and of mystic and spiritual literature can express profound truths about subsistent being. This type of writing lies outside the ambit of philosophy. But it does pertain to philosophy to show how the metaphorical and symbolical way of speaking is justified as a means of conveying genuine cognition in regard to subsistent existence. It is surely a task of the Christian philosopher to show that what is believed through supernatural faith is epistemologically applicable to subsistent existence, and to establish the way in which symbol and metaphor convey pertinent meaning in regard to something that transcends all material conditions and all limitation. They express in their own manner the perfection of their object, with the tacit understanding that the imperfection explicit in their notion be disregarded.

In these different ways, then, all perfections whatsoever are necessarily present within the subsistent perfection of all perfections, subsistent existence. They are present in it as perfections without imperfection. Really identical with subsistent existence, they leave no room for any limitation on the level on which they are now found. Were existence at all limited in its own notion to any class or order, it would be the actuality of that class to the exclusion of some other class or order. It would no longer coincide with its function of serving as the actuality of all actualities. As a finite object it would come under the original grasp of conceptualization, and would not have to be made known through a different kind of cognition, judgment. In a word, it would not fit in with the requirements of the actuality in which the existence of observable things consists. Existence, as originally grasped in sensible things, allows no limitation to arise from its own self. Where it is found just in itself, that is, where it subsists, it is accordingly unlimited. It is infinite perfection, and infinity of perfections, the infinity of all perfections.

Infinite perfection, therefore, is what pure actuality means when it is reached through reasoning from existence. But is this notion at all the same as the notion in Aristotle of actuality without potentiality, the notion from which the concept of pure actuality emerges historically? Has not the notion become very different from what it was in its original philosophic source? It does seem to be radically different. For the Stagirite, perfection meant form and finitude. It implied something finished and, accordingly, "perfect" in the etymological signification of the term. In this Aristotelian setting pure actuality would have to mean separate forms, each finite yet purely actual in itself.

What causes the great difference between these two philosophical notions of pure actuality? Is the difference not made imperative by their respective starting points? For Aristotle, the most basic actuality known is form, something that of its nature is finite or limited. Against this background the perpetuity of cosmic motion could be assured only by a final cause that had no potentiality at all, no potentiality that could ever allow the possibility of a break in the final causality. Such was the manner in which pure actuality was located in finite forms by the Stagirite. Where, however, a metaphysical procedure is based upon existence, all the forms, no matter how perfect, have their actuality from something else. They are, accordingly, potential in its regard. They all have to be actualized by existence, or else they are not actual. No object other than subsistent existence, therefore, can be regarded as pure actuality in this setting. Functioning above the limiting order of form, existence is not a finitizing principle. When subsistent just in itself, it contains nothing that could limit it. It already includes all subsistent perfection and, consequently, cannot allow any second instance of itself. Radically unlike pure actuality in Aristotle, it cannot be a multiplicity. While accepting the finitude of form as a perfection in relation to matter, procedure on the existential level regards form as in potency to a further actuality, namely existence, which is an actuality that in itself does not involve limitation. As a result it arrives at a radically different notion of pure actuality.

Does all this mean, then, that one may in one way or another predicate every possible perfection of subsistent being? Does it mean that everything one encounters in the world of experience manifests perfection that is already found in subsistent existence? Does one thereby actually know that one may read into the nature of subsistent existence every perfection of which one has had experience and every perfection that one is able to conceive?

The reasoning just concluded can mean nothing else. It has shown that every perfection whatsoever has to be actualized by existence, and, accordingly, is in fact actualized when its actuality, existence, subsists. Positively, then, may not one keep acquiring an ever increasing knowledge of subsistent existence? May not one continue seeing in it the perfections of everything one encounters? Will not this include reading back into it all the developments and advances in the historicity of human life? Need there be any end to the enterprise, as long as men keep engaged in metaphysics? In the infinity of subsistent existence the perfections of all these events, including the perfection of their distinguishing and differentiating marks, and of the ambitions and hopes and struggles vivified in them, are all contained.

But they are contained in it without any imperfection. They are in it, accordingly, without any change. Change necessarily involves potentiality and imperfection in its own very notion. It can therefore be applied only metaphorically to subsistent being. No real internal process, in consequence, can take place within subsistent existence. This is in sharp contrast with a Whiteheadian notion of reality in which process and development play the basic role. Rather, what is there in subsistent existence is completely there and always there. Anything new is already there, even in the very perfection that gives it its special attraction as new.

These considerations mean that the incompleteness involved in existence as first grasped in material things has been transcended. Only the actuality, the perfection remains. The imperfection has entirely disappeared when existence has been reached as a nature, and not as the actuation of something else. The incompleteness in which material existence is pinpointed to a present while emergent from the past and pregnant with a future, is obviously an imperfection. Such existence is not there all together. It is clearly lacking important parts, its past and its future. It actuates only to the extent its limited and essentially mobile subject, the material thing, permits. But when found subsistent in itself, it necessarily is actual to the full extent of its notion as the actuality of all actualities. Where it is a nature it absorbs all possible perfections into its own present unity. It is not spread out in time. Rather, existence is there contained in a duration that has no past and no future. Traditionally, this type of duration has been called eternity.

Correspondingly, subsistent existence can have no real relations with anything outside itself.[12] A real relation means real dependence upon a really different term. But real dependence on something else introduces an element of imperfection into the thing that is thereby related. Would not relations of this kind introduce real imperfection into subsistent existence? Would they not be incompatible with its nature, and entirely exclude it from its infinity of perfection? Really identical with existence, like everything else in subsistent being, would they not make subsistent being essentially subordinate to something else? In it they could not be present as accidents, they would have to be there as essential aspects. When one speaks of the relations of subsistent being to other things, then, one is speaking of mental constructs, as one con-

---

[12] For the case that it can have real relations in this regard, see Walter E. Stokes, "Is God Really Related to this World?" *Proceedings of the American Catholic Philosophical Association*, XXXIX (1965), 145–151.

ceives subsistent existence in relation to those things on account of their dependence upon it. The real dependence is in the other things, and not at all in subsistent existence, just as the relation of the table in front of you, to your knowledge, is not something really in the table itself; on the contrary, it is a construct of your mind.

To sum up, one can know *that* existence subsists, and *that* all other perfections are contained in it, without knowing either *what* subsistent existence is or *what* any of the other perfections are on that level. The situation has given rise to both the positive and the negative theologies of Christian tradition. It has brought into literature the puzzling label "the mystery of being."[13] Should not the sense in which existence is a mystery emerge from the foregoing considerations? As originally grasped in judgment can it be termed mysterious at all? Is it not open to every observer? Is it not everywhere obvious? Could anything be clearer, more knowable, more evident, than the fact that things around us exist? Is not the existence of these things fully as evident as their color, their size, their relations to and differences from one another? As grasped through judgment, does existence take on the aspect of mystery any more than do quantity and motion? These aspects are obvious, not mysterious, even though they are pregnant with the far-reaching sciences of mathematics and mechanics. Like them, existence as originally known is something obvious, workaday, and quite down to earth. Anybody knows what you mean when you say of cabbages or kings that they exist.

However, when one conceptualizes what one has grasped through judgment, the situation changes. If one looks for new and characteristic content in the concept, is not one truly baffled? There is no such content there. Yet existence is eminently meaningful. Should it not therefore manifest a rich and

---

[13] E.g., Gabriel Marcel, *The Mystery of Being*, tr. René Hague (Chicago: Henry Regnery, 1951).

distinctive content? If the process by which the concept of existence is formed is not clearly understood, will not these two facets appear irreconcilable? Will not the concept, accordingly, be regarded as having a mysterious object? Does not the concept of existence become in this way a pseudo-mystery?

Real mystery, notwithstanding, is encountered when one reaches subsistent existence. Here one has arrived at the *nature* of existence, while at the same time fully aware of complete inability to know *what* existence is. Yet the nature of anything is what the thing is. Accordingly, one knows *that* subsistent existence is a nature, but that one cannot know it in the manner of a nature. One can have no genuine conceptual knowledge of it. In this way it thoroughly meets the qualifications for a mystery. One knows that it is there, and at the same time realizes that all hope of knowing anything about what it is is futile. A murder mystery may present enough clues to allow the crime to be diagnosed as murder, but few enough to preclude the possibility of ever attaining any further knowledge of motive or criminal. It has to remain a mystery. Correspondingly, in a remote enough way of course, the existence of observable things offers sufficient clues to establish subsistent existence as the infinity of all perfections. Yet what the existence itself is, or what any of the perfections are when they are identified with it, is destined to remain a mystery. The nature of existence, in a word, is shrouded in mystery, even though the occurrence of existence in observable things is obvious.

This situation gives rise to an important anomaly in regard to the predication of being. In the case of the objects in the categories, one grasps through conceptualization a nature in abstraction from all the instances of which it may be predicated. Abstracted from all instances, the common nature is not an instantiation of itself. The common nature "animal," for instance, is not an animal, nor is the common nature "man" a man. With regard to existence, however, the case is significantly different. Its nature is not isolated through conceptual abstraction, but is reasoned to from what is grasped through judgment. In this way its nature is found to be completely identical with a subsistent agent. The nature of existence, accordingly, is an instantiation of existence. Against an Aristotelian background it may be called the primary instance of existence.

Is not subsistent existence therefore a being, an existent? The nature of existence is itself a thing that exists. In this respect it cannot be equated with the other objects of predication, objects that are originally grasped through conceptualization. The tendency to concentrate all the perfection of a common object within a single and separate instance may be seen developed in the Platonic doctrine of Ideas. Its rejection for all objects without exception may be found in Aristotle. Metaphysical reasoning based upon existence has room for both procedures, and has need for them both. It requires that the nature of existence be an instantiation of itself, and that likewise each of the transcendental perfections should be its own primary instance. In all other objects, on the contrary, the common nature does not instantiate itself.

Existence, then, is indeed a nature, but it is found as a nature in only one instantiation of itself, its primary instance. In all other instances it is not a nature, but an actuality other than anything in the nature of the thing it is actuating. Generic and specific concepts, on the other hand, represent perfections that are present as natures in all their instances. To equate existence from this standpoint with the object of a generic or specific concept is to ask for much trouble, leading finally to the conclusion that no nature remains for existence.[14]

---

[14] See Chapter I, n. 5, for the claim that no nature is left for existence, since it is set apart from the notes that make up a thing's definition. Here the way of reaching the nature can be only through reasoning in the line of efficient causality to subsistent existence, and through subsistent existence to

To understand the process by which existence has gradually been crowded off the stage in the Western philosophical enterprise, and to be able to defend its right to a new hearing, must not one be keenly aware that the nature of existence is not reached through the abstraction of any formal element or through reasoning in the line of formal elements? Must not one realize clearly it is a nature that is knowable only through reasoning based upon the sequence of efficient causality, through reasoning from observable existence to a primary efficient cause?

---

the perfections contained in the nature. In the step of reasoning to a cause other than the original existent, moreover, one is not following the Aristotelian model sense of demonstrating a property of the nature. One is proving something of another thing, namely that the other thing exists.

CHAPTER V

Bestowal of Existence

It is one thing to start with the observed existence of sensible things and reason to subsistent existence as their first efficient cause. But is it not quite another to attempt any reasoning in the opposite direction? From the viewpoint of its nature, subsistent existence remains entirely unknown, utterly unknown, to the human mind. The nature of existence, accordingly, stays impenetrable. How, then, could one hope to make it the starting point of a reasoning processs, in the way one reasons from the nature of a triangle to the equality of the angles with two right angles? Is it not obviously impossible?

Not knowing the nature of subsistent existence, therefore, one is not in a position to conclude from it that anything else exists. Nor is one able to understand, from within, the activity by which it bestows existence upon other things. On the philosophical level the characteristic activity of subsistent existence, the production of the effect that corresponds in other things to its nature, namely, the giving of existence, is impervious to human understanding. One can start from existent things and reason to subsistent existence. But one is completely unable to start with subsistent existence and reason to the fact that other things exist. There is no authentic concept of existence to provide the basis for the reasoning.

Furthermore, is not this consideration heightened by the freedom with which subsistent existence is identified through and through? One knows that all perfections are really identified, are one, in subsistent existence. Need there be any hesitation in accepting freedom as a perfection, in contrast to constrained or predetermined activity? Moreover, existence in itself involves no individual, specific, or general limitations.[1] When it is subsistent, consequently, it is not determined by any essential specifications, by any fixed framework. It is freedom itself. There is nothing in its nature to determine any set sequence of effects from it. Even aside from the viewpoint of human knowledge, its nature does not in fact predetermine its effects, in the way the nature of a triangle is the ground for conclusions drawn in geometry and trigonometry. To call subsistent existence "the ground of being" is rather misleading. It is in no sense a ground upon which the consequences necessarily follow. It is their cause, in the sense of the agent that produced them, as has been seen in the preceding chapter. But that sense is hardly conveyed by the notion of "ground," with its implication of consequences that follow in the sequence of formal causality.[2]

Yet the prospect of understanding things in the light of their highest causes traditionally has been the goal of philosophy. Is one now cut off from any understanding of things through knowledge of their first efficient cause? Certainly, if one knows that the existence of observable things, because it

---

[1] See Chapter III, n. 14; Chapter IV, n. 2.

[2] There is something quite strained in applying the notion of "ground" to an efficient cause. One can hardly call a cabinetmaker, for instance, the "ground" of a table. In general, an efficient cause produces rather than grounds its effects. In Plotinus and Spinoza, however, there is necessary sequence of things from their first principle. In Leibniz the goodness of the first principle requires the production of the best possible world.

is prior to and accidental to their natures, is being imparted
to them by subsistent existence, one thereby knows something
about the activity of subsistent being. Can that knowledge
be harnessed in ways that will generate philosophical insight
into the bestowal of existence?

In the long Christian Neoplatonic tradition, the bestowal
of existence by the first efficient cause was brought under the
general notion of "participation." As a technical philosophical
concept, sharing or participation goes back at least to the
Greek philosopher Anaxagoras, and possibly to Parmenides.[3]
It became highly developed in the Platonic doctrine of Ideas.
In these Greek thinkers, however, it is found solely in a setting
of formal causality. A form, such as humanity, or heat, or
justice, was seen as shared by a number of instances. They were
accordingly regarded as participating in the form or as par-
taking of it, as though each had a part or share of the form.
But carried over to the realm of efficient causality, must not
the notion of participation become considerably different?
Can it any longer be a question of envisaging a nature that is
present as a nature in a number of different individuals? It
can hardly be the notion of a form whose various parts or
shares are found scattered throughout its instances. It is rather
the notion of an agent that brings into existence not parts
or shares of its own nature, but things that have other natures
entirely. There is in this case no one nature that is shared as
a nature. Strictly, there is no formal cause here that is found
commonly in all.[4] Formal elements, on the contrary, are made

---

[3] See Anaxagoras, *Fragments*, 6, 11, and 12 (DK, 59B); Parmenides,
Fragments, 9.4 (DK, 28B).

[4] On rare occasions existence is referred to as a "form" by St. Thomas
Aquinas. See "*quandoque forma significata per nomen est ipsum esse*" ("sometimes the form signified by a name is existence itself"). *In I Sententiarum*,
d. 35, q. 1, a. 4, Solut.; ed. Mandonnet, I, 819. ". . . *forma a qua imponitur,
scilicet esse*" (". . . the form from which it is applied, namely existence")
ibid., d. 25, q. 1, a. 4, Solut.; I, 612. Similarly God is referred to as "form,"
ibid., d. 2, q. 1, a. 2, Solut.; I, 62. This latter way of speaking may be seen
also in *Summa Theologiae*, I, 3, 2c (3o). See also the use of "forma" in

to exist. The procedure consists in production by efficient causality, and not in any sharing of a common nature by way of formal causality.

Although in the present case existence is the nature of the efficient cause, the imparting of existence does not mean here that the nature of the effects and the nature of the cause have any formal characteristics in common. On the level attainable by philosophy, on which subsistent existence cannot be differentiated by any generic or specific trait or by reception into an individual subject, how could any characteristic be formally shared? From a metaphysical viewpoint, all things upon which existence is bestowed are the effects of subsistent existence, the products of subsistent existence, the work of subsistent existence, without making manifest any note that would call for the sharing in a common formal aspect. The imparting of existence means solely that natures radically different from subsistent existence are made to exist. Here the nature of the cause is existence, while the nature of the effects is not existence at all but in every case something other than existence. If in any case existence were a characteristic of a thing's nature, it would straightway identify the thing wholly and entirely with subsistent being, as the reasoning of Parmenides makes clear. Existence in the status of a nature will necessarily

---

the initial *argumenta* 1–5 of *In Boethii de Trinitate*, VI, 3, and in the citing of Boethius at the end of the body of the article; ed. Decker, pp. 218.22–219.21; 223.16. On the other hand, of course, existence is found sharply distinguished from form: "*Non enim est esse rei neque forma ejus neque materia ipsius*" ("For the existence of a thing is neither its form nor its matter") *De Substantis Separatis*, c. VIII, no. 44; ed. F. J. Lescoe, p. 80. The Boethian *essendi forma* is deliberately changed to *actum essendi, In Boethii de Hebdomadibus*, c. II; ed. Mandonnet, *Opuscula*, I, 172. The necessity of expressing what is beyond form in terms of form has become noticeable in the current movement of structuralism. On the claim that "all thought that tries to define the inadequacy of form becomes form in its turn," and that in this respect man is "stretched out on the procrustean bed of Form," see the "Editor's Introduction" to the double volume devoted to structuralism, *Yale French Studies*, XXXVI–XXXVII (1966), pp. 5 and 8. A double issue of *Revue Internationale de Philosophie*, XIX (1965), nos. 3–4, was likewise given to the topic.

subsist and embrace all the rest in its infinite perfection. The Eleatic deductions on the all-inclusive scope of being apply cogently here.

What light do these considerations throw upon the bestowal of existence? They focus attention sharply enough on the conclusion that all things upon which existence is bestowed are natures really different from subsistent existence. Into these natures existence cannot enter as a note. Existence has to be given them by an efficient cause. As far as they themselves are concerned, they are merely able to receive it. Even this statement of the case is difficult. Without existence they are not there to receive anything. The statement is made from the viewpoint of the role played by the thing itself as it is actuated by existence. Since the existence is the actuation, what is thereby actuated comes under the opposite term, potentiality. Taken from Aristotle, as noted earlier,[5] actuality meant form. The matter actuated by the form was termed potentiality. It was the capacity to receive a form, for instance the capacity of wood to take on the form of a table. Transferred to the order of existence, the actuation of a nature different from existence requires, similarly, that the nature function as a potentiality to the existence. But is there not an obvious disparity in the two cases? Form can presuppose its corresponding potentiality, matter, as already there. Existence, however, cannot presuppose the thing it makes exist. In being imparted, then, existence gives rise to the potentiality it actuates.

This requirement in the bestowal of existence leads to important knowledge about it. It shows that the bestowal of existence is always upon something really other than the existence imparted. If the existence became really identified with the nature it actuates, it would function there as a nature and, accordingly would absorb the alleged new thing into the

---

[5] See Chapter III, n. 3.

unicity of subsistent existence. Anything produced, therefore, cannot be subsistent existence; nor can it be really identical with its own existence. In Thomistic tradition this distinction of every caused thing from its existence has been known as the real distinction between essence and existence. It is the real distinction between a thing and its being. While inspection of observable natures shows that human reason has to place between them a distinction made by itself insofar as they are objects of two different cognitive activities, the demonstration that in subsistent being existence is a real nature embracing all perfections requires the further conclusion that the bestowal of real existence is always upon something really different from the existence thereby imparted.

Another important conclusion is the limiting role played by the thing produced. In order to be imparted, existence has to actuate a nature really other than itself. But natures other than existence are finite, limited, knowable as the determinate objects of conceptualization. They are natures such as those of a metal, a tree, a cat, a man. In being made to exist, they acquire the existence of the metal, or of the tree, and so on in each case. The existence of the one is not the existence of the other, as is clearly known through judgment in the case of many of the accidental characteristics and, outside the hypothesis of complete physical monism, can be reasoned to fairly cogently in regard to the things themselves. This means that existence, by its very bestowal on something, is thereby limited by the confines prescribed by the thing's nature. The limitation is required for its bestowal, since without the limitation it would remain really and completely identified with subsistent existence.

In this way the imagery in the notion of something receiving existence is broken through. What is meant is that the existence bestowed by an efficient cause involves necessarily a limiting potency really different from itself. It could not issue from the efficient cause except as actuating that potency. In the case of observable agents, the correspondence between effect and cause is on the level of nature and occasions no surprise. A carpenter makes a table, mice propagate mice. But where the nature is existence itself, effect and cause cannot correspond in nature. Existence as a nature cannot be bestowed on anything. It was reached by a demonstration showing that all caused existence is accidental to nature and issues from uncaused existence, and this existence although here a nature, is not bestowed upon a subject. A thing whose existence is caused, then, inevitably must be of a different nature from existence itself. The characteristic effect of subsistent existence, it is true, cannot be other than existence. But is the new existence *what* is produced? No. What is produced is a galaxy, a metal, a tree, an animal, a man. To issue from subsistent existence, the new existence has to be the existence of a finite thing such as these. Each new existence, accordingly, involves a potency that limits it and remains other than it. The potency is the thing that is produced.

Does not this explain the imagery of a reception of existence? The thing is not there first, to receive existence, but is involved in the new existence as the subject actuated by it as it proceeds from the efficient cause. Just as a subject may be spoken of as receiving formal actuation when it acquires a new color or size, so for convenience the existential actuation may be regarded as having been received by the subject, even though the subject was not there antecedently to receive it.

The subject, accordingly, is what limits existential actuality to the existence of this or that finite object. As a limiting potency the subject, in its turn, has to remain entitatively other than its own existence, if it is to be kept from absorption into subsistent being. In the real world existence has to stay really outside the natures of finite things. Correspondingly, in cognitional existence there has to be entitative distinction between thing and being. In a word, existence can never be bestowed upon anything else as a nature. It can be imparted only as the actuality of a nature other than itself. That is what is meant, from the existential viewpoint, in saying that a thing is made or produced.

The real distinction of nature from existence in observable things finally uncovers the basis for the difference between the two fundamental types of human intellection. Through conceptualization or simple apprehension a thing is known in terms of its nature. Through judgment it is known from the viewpoint of its existence. Similarly, the reason emerges why conceptualization can never be separated from a simultaneous act of judgment, and vice versa. The reason is that in things nature can never be found without existence, nor existence without nature.

To complete the picture, finitude is a characteristic that has to condition everything outside subsistent existence. Of itself, of its own nature, a finite thing has no being whatsoever because it is radically other than existence. Each finite thing is of itself just nothing. Only through actuation by existence does it become something. From this standpoint its function is only to be a limitation of the existence bestowed upon it, even though from the standpoint of the perfection so actuated it is something very positive, such as a stone or an oak or a man. Yet to be known as man or oak or stone, the respective existence of each, either real or cognitional, has to be presupposed.

In any production, accordingly, existence is bestowed upon something that otherwise has no being. Even in the case of artifacts or other accidents, the product did not exist prior to the activity of the efficient cause. Could one say, for instance, that a table existed before the cabinetmaker produced it? The wood was there, but the table was not. Is not the most one can say just this, that the table was capable of being produced, able to be made? But is that not the same as saying that in itself it is but a potency for existence, in the sense just considered? Where matter is presupposed, then, it receives new existence under a new form, either substantial or accidental. Where no material is presupposed, as has to be the case in the first production of things by subsistent existence, the production has been given traditionally a special name. It is called creation, regardless of whether it is viewed as a temporal beginning or as an actuation that never commenced in time. In either case, all things other than subsistent existence are traditionally called creatures in this setting, even though they come into existence long after the original act of creation, and through generation or other kinds of efficient causality.

However, the metaphysical reasoning from the prior and accidental character of existence in observable things has led directly to the imparting of existence here and now, rather than to previous creation. All things, insofar as they have existence accidental to themselves, are being given it by an efficient cause. The argument is immediately concerned with a causal influx that is taking place at exactly the present moment. No matter how things may have received their existence when they first came into being, are they not constantly receiving it from a cause as long as they continue in existence? Was not that the import of the original reasoning to an efficient cause?

This continuous causality that sustains things in existence has been technically known as conservation. With regard to existence that originated immediately through creation, it may be looked upon as a continuation of the creative activity. In this case the supposition of an intermediate series of causes between the effect and subsistent existence disappears. Where intermediate causes produce a thing, on the other hand, they may play a corresponding part in its conservation. Conservation of a thing's existence, just as its initial acquisition of existence, may accordingly proceed either mediately or immediately from subsistent being, as far as the cogency of the reasoning to subsistent existence is concerned.

But how can anything finite be an agent that imparts existence? Is not the thing's nature radically other than existence? How then can existence correspond to it as an effect? Does not the fact of efficient causality in finite agents have to be painstakingly established after Hume's incisive critique of our knowledge regarding it?[6] Can even the possibility of finite efficient causality be taken for granted in the face of the attacks made against it by the various types of Occasionalism? Is there any per se absurdity in Malebranche's claim of a contradiction in the notion "that all the angels and demons joined together are able to rustle a straw"?[7]

On the other hand, however, is one not immediately conscious of being the efficient cause of one's own internal activities such as intellection and free choosing? The fact seems as immediate and as clear as any other. Can it be denied or set aside, without conclusive proof that one is victim of an illusion in thinking that one is really performing one's own internal activities? Moreover, even though observation of efficient causality in other things is denied us, is not credulity strained in trying to believe that these things are equipped with so much complicated apparatus to all appearances geared to produce effects yet never do produce any? Must one hold as mere window dressing the complicated and exact adaptations in key, ignition, explosion of the mixture, the pistons, the crankshaft, and rest of the intricate machinery involved in making the car go? Is all this elaborate series but a symbolic

---

[6] See Chapter IV, n. 4.

[7] Nicolas Malebranche, *Entretiens sur la Métaphysique et sur la Religion*, VII, 10; ed. P. Fontana (Paris: 1922), I, 154. For a penetrating discussion of Malebranche's Occasionalism as "first of all a metaphysical account of finite being or existence," and critique of the leading interpretations it has received, see Beatrice K. Rome, *The Philosophy of Malebranche* (Chicago: The University of Chicago Press, 1963), pp. 161–242.

token that subsistent existence, and subsistent existence alone, is there at work? Surely there is at least enough prima facie enticement to investigate the possibility that things other than subsistent being can function as genuine efficient causes.

First of all, when anything new is produced, something that did not exist before is brought into being. There is a new thing, there is new existence. But every finite thing is limited to what exists within it. How could anything that did not yet exist be "unpacked" from its content? Yet whenever a new effect is produced, its actuality, its actual self, was not there previously. Its ultimate explanation, accordingly, cannot be found in any finite cause. The new effect, in the perfection of its own existence, is just not found in a finite cause. Only in the infinite perfection of subsistent existence is the perfection of all possible effects, past, present, and future, to be found. Unless subsistent existence, then, is at work as an agent in the production of a new effect, the very possibility of efficient causality cannot be explained.

But does this consideration rule out the possibility of finite efficient causes? Hardly. It does show cogently that the ultimate explanation of efficient causality in the production of a new effect has to lie in subsistent existence. In this respect subsistent existence always has to be the primary agent, the primary efficient cause. But do not two possibilities stand open? On the one hand, the primary agent could produce the effect immediately, as in the case of the original production of things through creation. On the other hand, it could produce further things through the mediation of those already created. One person may speak to others directly through the natural sound waves, or indirectly through electronic activity of telephone or radio. One starts one's car through the activity of spark and explosive mixture and pressure upon pistons and shaft. Is there any contradiction, then, in the notion of doing something through the activity of something else?

But even if there is not a contradiction in the general notion of doing something through another's activity, may there not be a contradiction of some kind in the particular case of bestowing existence through the activity of something else? The new existence, it is true, is finite. But even so, how can it originate in any way from the finite cause, a cause limited strictly to its own existence and perfection? It could at the most be conceived as passing through the finite cause, not originating from it. But surely that would not be enough to term the finite thing an efficient cause. To be an efficient cause, does it not have to actively produce the new existence? Besides, what could the notion that the new existence passes through the finite cause hope to mean? Clearly, the new existence is found only in the thing it makes exist, and in a pre-contained way in the infinite perfection of subsistent being.

Undoubtedly the problem here is bristling with difficulties. The fundamental obstacle is that without an authentic concept of existence the human mind cannot approach it from within, but only from the side of the effects. The fact that finite things can be active may be considered as established from one's own internal experience of conscious activity. It is as clear and compelling as any other fact that comes within the purview of human cognition. That observable things in the real world are themselves active, for instance elementary particles in their swift travel, a seed in growing, a rodent in gnawing, a wrestler in throwing his opponent, seems to be the only acceptable hypothesis and to be mandatory as a presumption.[8] The philosophical problem, accordingly, is not to show that finite

---

[8] Even with Hume the question bore not so much upon the presence of efficient causality as upon the means at the disposal of the human mind for knowing it. Cf.: ". . . I have never asserted so absurd a Proposition as that anything might arise without a Cause: I have only maintain'd, that our Certainty of the Falsehood of that Proposition proceeded neither from Intuition nor Demonstration: but from another Source." Hume, in The Letters of David Hume, ed. J. Y. T. Greig (Oxford: Oxford University Press, 1932), I, 187.

things are efficient causes. Rather, with that tenet accepted, the problem is to explain how they can be efficient causes even though all new existence originates in the activity of subsistent being.

With the presumption, then, that finite things are in fact efficient causes, one may begin by asking what characteristics in the effect manifest strict correspondence with the finite agent. In the case of the generation of living things, could the correspondence in nature be more clear? Maple trees propagate maples, mice generate mice. The specific perfection in question is adequately found in the finite causes. With regard to artifacts, the technical training and skill is found in the artisan, corresponding to the effect induced into the material. Physical and chemical forces everywhere correspond to definite effects, making engineering and other such accomplishments possible. In one way or another, the finite causes are adequate in nature to the effects they produce. But they cannot produce the effects without thereby giving them existence .

Is it not impossible, therefore, to accept finite agents as efficient causes of a thing's nature without simultaneously seeing them as the cause of the thing's existence? Do the two not go together? What sense would it make to say that the finite agent was the cause of the thing's nature while subsistent existence was the cause of its being? Clearly, the two cannot be separated. What causes the one causes the other. If the finite agent produces the thing, it inevitably causes the thing's existence. If the primary efficient cause originates the existence of the thing, by the same token it produces the thing's nature. What one can know, consequently, about existence and about finite efficient causality seems to require the concurrence of two causes, one from the viewpoint of producing the new thing, the other from the viewpoint of originating the new existence. Yet each of these two causes has to produce the nature as well as the existence of the effect.

Traditionally, the term used for this requirement of two causes has in fact been "concurrence."[9] With subsistent existence designated as the first efficient cause, the finite agents, accordingly, were known as secondary causes. The terminology is convenient. On the presumption that the efficient causality of the secondary causes is accepted as at work, one can speak of the concurrence of the primary cause as necessary for the activity of every finite agent. How? Where the activity of the finite agent is not always taking place throughout the course of the agent's existence, as for instance it was taking place with Descartes in his contention that the human mind was always thinking,[10] the agent has to be brought into activity from inactivity. This obviously is the work of some other agent, since it is presupposed to any activity on the part of the agent that otherwise would be inactive. It can be caused immediately by a finite agent, as when a man strikes a match and the flame lights a candle. Ultimately, however, like any efficient causality, it will have to be caused by subsistent existence. Since this type of concurrence is prior to the activity of the finite agent, it has been technically called antecedent concurrence.[11]

But is antecedent concurrence sufficient to meet the difficulties just sketched? Is one big push by the first cause enough to account for the outward surge of the galaxies through the millenia, dispensing with any supplementary influx? Is the single big bang able to keep the elementary particles in swift motion throughout the ages? Is the one stroke of the cue

---

[9] The technical Scholastic designation is *concursus*. Discussions of the theme may be found in Neoscholastic manuals, e.g., Josef Hontheim, *Institutiones Theodicaeae* (Freiburg i. Breigau, 1893), pp. 770–803; Juan José Urráburu, *Institutiones Philosophicae* (Paris & Rome, 1891–1908), VIII, 743–1038; Josef Gredt, *Elementa Philosophiae Aristotelico-Thomisticae* (7th ed. Freiburg i. Breisgau, 1937), II, 246–271 (nos. 835–848).

[10] Descartes, *Quintae Responsiones*, A-T, VII, 356.23–357.6; *Ad Hyperaspistem*, August 1641, A-T, III, 423.16–17.

[11] An acceptable Scholastic term is *concursus praevius*. *Praemotio physica* is inept, *praedeterminatio* is misleading.

capable of making all the pool balls reach the required pockets?

As far as the knowledge and wisdom and power of the first efficient cause are concerned, no problem arises. These are all infinite in their respective types of perfection, and therefore fully able to control to the smallest detail everything that happens in the universe. The difficulty lies elsewhere. Just as the reasoning to subsistent being showed not only that observable things had to be produced originally by subsistent existence, but also, and primarily, that they are being kept in existence by its present influx, so the reasoning also requires that their activities be sustained by the continued influx of the first cause. This implies that finite production, originally set afoot by the first cause, can keep proceeding only through ever-present activation by subsistent being. In this particular type of influx there is no longer question of the finite agent taking an active part. Rather, is not the first cause alone producing the action from the viewpoint of its existence, while the secondary cause is simultaneously producing the same action from the standpoint of its nature? And, where the action consists in the production of a distinct effect, will not the first cause be accounting for the existence of the effect, while the secondary cause accounts for its nature? Both together produce the effect. Each produces the whole effect, nature and existence combined, but each from its own standpoint.

Do not these considerations sufficiently meet the difficulties just raised? There is now no need of requiring the new existence to pass through the finite agent. The simultaneous concurrence of the first cause with the finite agent's activity amply suffices for the production of new existence in the effect. In producing the effect's nature, to which the finite cause is proportioned, this secondary agent is enabled to produce it as existent, by means of the concomitant activity of the first cause.[12] Rather than the image of new existence passing

---

[12] For the tenet that the secondary agent is literally the efficient cause of the new existence, though causing it "*in virtute agentis primi,*" see St. Thomas,

through the secondary cause, the image of the two different causes concurring on different levels is required.

This means, then, that the concurrence of the primary efficient cause is twofold. The created cause, which is not its own action, has to be brought from inactivity to activity. This can be done by the primary cause either immediately or mediately, and may be designated as antecedent concurrence. That is the first type of concurrence required. The second type is the immediate activity of the primary cause in producing new existence. This type of concurrence has to function simultaneously with the finite causality. Unlike the antecedent concurrence, it bears immediately upon the finite action and effect, and not upon the finite cause. In this way it is functioning simultaneously with, and not antecedently to, the secondary agent. For that reason it is known technically as simultaneous concurrence.[13]

Since the absolutely new existence that is caused in any production could never be contained within the limits of an intermediate cause, which as finite can exist only as itself and nothing else, the simultaneous concurrence cannot be given in any mediate fashion. Always it has to be immediate on the

---

Summa Contra Gentiles, III, 66, *Amplius ultimum* and *Item secundum*. Here the notion "*in virtute*" signifies the role of an instrument under the active dominance of the principal cause, as when a typewriter prints legible typescript under the pounding of a stenographer. The image, however, breaks down on two scores. In concurring, the primary cause is immediately attaining the effect in producing the new existence. On the other hand, the secondary agent is a principal cause of the effect from the standpoint of the effect's nature, and not just an instrument. Cf. St. Thomas, *De Potentia*, III, 7.

Although it is easier to use the expression "the first cause" or "the primary cause," there is nothing grammatically odd about the expression "subsistent existence produces effects." The adjective "subsistent" marks the existence as a thing in itself and, accordingly, able to perform activities. For this reason there should be much less objection than in expressions like "the incarnate wisdom counsels us" or "Yankee ingenuity discovered a solution."

[13] Cf.: ". . . since God is the first cause of all things, his power (*virtus*) is most immediate to them all. But as he himself is his power, he therefore not only is the immediate principle of operation in all, but is immediately operating in all." St. Thomas, *In I Sententiarum*, d. 37, q. 1, a. 1, ad 4m; I, 859.

part of the primary cause. The primary cause, accordingly, is always operating in every finite activity, immediately causing the activity from the viewpoint of its existence, while the secondary agent is causing the same activity from the viewpoint of the activity's nature. By the same token the primary cause is acting immediately upon every product, causing it immediately from the standpoint of existence.

All this explanation, of course, does not achieve any understanding of the bestowal of existence from within. For that an authentic concept of existence would be required. What it does purport to do, however, is to account for the production of new existence in terms of what is known by the human mind about efficient causation and about the existence in observable things that is grasped through judgment. It is on the basis of these data alone that metaphysical reasoning has to work out an acceptable explanation of the way existence is bestowed. Though not proceeding from within, it is capable of profound development and continued application in the understanding of man's daily life and his engagement in characteristically human concerns.[14] It shows even more clearly than before[15] why the notion of subsistent existence as the "ground of being" is so highly inappropriate. Far from merely grounding, the first cause actively produces effects. It is at work within the activity of every finite cause, enabling causes limited in being to their own finite selves to produce utterly new existence that till then was not at all present in the created universe.

These considerations, then, show that in every natural or human activity subsistent existence is itself present and active in the production of the effect from the viewpoint of the existential dimension. The drawing of a breath, the pointing

---

[14] For instance, it explains on the metaphysical level the scriptural teaching, "In him we live and move and have our being," *The New Testament, The Acts of the Apostles*, 17:28 (RSV).

[15] Supra, n. 2.

of a finger, the thinking of the least thought, all involve the intimate activity of the first efficient cause. In this respect the activity of the primary cause is definitely from within, not from without. Only in virtue of this intimate concurring activity are secondary causes able to produce effects. Only because within their own activity at its deepest and most intimate existential center subsistent existence is incessantly at work, are they able to bring new things into existence.

The need for concurrence by an agent of infinite nature becomes intensified in the problem of human freedom. Does not the role of infinite power, or omnipotence, become indispensable? Free choice is a fact for human internal experience. One has immediate knowledge that one is choosing freely. In deciding to pick up the pen from the table, one is fully aware that it is in one's power to lift it up or to leave it on the table. Nothing that has gone before determines the activity to be the one or the other. But how can any limited power hope to give the full and final explanation of this type of action?

Even though the agent, the man, is limited and determined in nature, the activity of free choice transcends determination and limitation to anything definite. Not only from the viewpoint of its existence, but also from that of its type, does not this activity of free choice require an unlimited cause? Does it not have to originate in an activity that knows no limitations?[16] Does not the free choice, if it is to be entirely free, have to be caused by omnipotent activity? But that activity is identical with the freedom that is subsistent existence, an actuality absolutely undetermined by any limitation. In this way do not the notions of freedom in itself and of subsistent existence entirely coincide? Is not the one in reality the other? Accordingly, all participated freedom, as in the case of man

[16] Cf.: "And to say that God does not cause freedom or that there is no freedom is to say pretty much the same thing." Gerard Smith, *Freedom in Molina* (Chicago, 1966), p. 225.

where free action is not the agent's essence, has to come from subsistent freedom, just as surely as all participated existence has to come from subsistent existence. And the reason is the same. Only in the primary cause do existence and freedom have the status of a nature.

All the determining of the freely chosen course of activity without doubt has to be done by the finite agent. It is the finite agent that makes the decision. The activity of the primary and infinite agent causes the secondary agent to do the determining, but does not itself determine the course of action. How is that possible? It is not something that the human mind can understand from the inside. Lacking an authentic concept of existence, the mind has no conceptual basis for penetrating this infinite type of activity. The mind can reason that every finite agent, because determined and limited in nature, determines the effect it produces to some definite and limited character. But subsistent existence, because absolutely unlimited in nature, does not operate under this restriction. It operates above the levels both of contingency and necessity.[17] It need not necessitate or constrain to anything, even when causing the activity of the finite agent down to the least detail.

This omnipotent type of activity cannot be understood from within by the human mind. But it can be investigated in terms of the starting points available to human intelligence. The objections arising from its equation with the essentially limited activity of finite agents can be obviated. The rest of the explanation has to be poised on the nature of the primary

---

[17] Cf.: ". . . the divine will must be understood as existing outside of the order of beings, as a cause producing the whole of being and all its differences. Now the possible and the necessary are differences of being, and therefore necessity and contingency in things and the distinction of each according to the nature of their proximate causes originate from the divine will itself, . . . a first cause, which transcends the order of necessity and contingency." St. Thomas, In I Perihermeneias, lect. 14, Leonine no. 22; tr. Jean T. Oesterle. Other texts from St. Thomas on the topic may be found gathered in G. Smith, op. cit., pp. 59–66.

efficient cause, which is unlimited and, accordingly, able to act
without determining. As in everything else about subsistent
existence, the means at the disposal of human thought allow
only the conclusion *that* it has to be so, without revealing *what*
the activity is. One knows that human freedom is caused freedom, caused free choice. The two notions would be incompatible if both agents were finite, but they are complementary,
and necessarily so, where one of the agents is finite and the
other infinite.

Omnipotence, accordingly, is required as a cause of free
activity in finite things. It means power unlimited by any
essential restrictions. Does its notion cause any special difficulties? Power to do things is a perfection. Like every other
perfection, it is found in infinite degree in subsistent existence.
There it is really identical with infinite being and, consequently, is unlimited in its character as power. No special
difficulty seems to arise in establishing the notion as one of
the perfections of subsistent being. Is not the perfection of
all possible effects already contained within this primary efficient cause? What could prevent its power, then, from extending to them all? Why should there be more of a problem
in bringing any one of them into existence rather than
another? As long as an essence is able to be projected, it is
capable of receiving existence from the primary cause.

Hardly necessary to remark, a combination of notions like
a square circle is not an essence. It is not a potentiality for
real existence. It is not a possible effect in the real world. The
only type of existence it can have is cognitional being in the
intellect. Quite similarly, one essential trait may exclude the
presence of a contrary trait in the same subject, as rationality
would exclude equinity in the same animal nature. These are
limitations that are implicit in finite essences. They allow mental projections that furnish no possibility of real existence. But
wherever there is possibility of existence, the power of the first

cause has its scope. It extends to all possibilities. That is just
what is meant by genuine omnipotence.[18]

With omnipotence so assessed, there should not be too much
difficulty in understanding that it is in full play throughout
the whole universe. In one way or another, it is causing all new
existence that appears in the real or cognitional worlds. Clearly,
it bestows existence in different ways. To a fleeting cloud
formation or to the warble of a canary's song existence is imparted in a way other than in the case of the enduring existence of the planets or of trees and animals. Existence is received in and limited and determined by the nature it actuates.
Functioning as potentiality to existence, the nature that is
actuated provides the reason why existence is bestowed in a
particular way. Where a nature has a material element that
can acquire and lose different forms, the existence is imparted
in accord with this contingent union between matter and
form. It is imparted in a contingent way. It may be called
contingent existence. The existence of a color that may be
lost by its subject, the existence of a compound that by elec-
trolysis can be changed into ions, the existence of plants and
animals that require organic structure, will be conferred in the
way these respective natures demand. The natures, on account
of their material element, are capable of dissolution. The potentiality into which existence is received conditions in this
way the existential actuation. All these things are able to lose
their existence. It is bestowed upon them contingently.

Contingent existence, accordingly, is found wherever the
things that exist are composites of matter and form. This type
of existence is gained and lost in the clash of acid against
base, of cat against mouse, of nation against nation, as each
seeks activity or nourishment or diversion or lebensraum at the

---

[18] On the meanings of omnipotence, see the papers on the topic by Paul
G. Kuntz, John Macquarrie, and William J. Wainwright, in *Proceedings of
the Seventh Inter-American Congress of Philosophy* (Quebec, 1967), I,
138–149.

expense of its counterparts. Throughout all the jungle clash, however, runs an evolutionary progress that has brought the things to their present cosmic, organic, and cultural stage. With the noosphere the presence of intelligence, with its consequent ability to choose freely, has to be faced squarely and scrutinized dispassionately. Is there not a profound difference in the way in which intelligence functions, when compared with non-intelligent material things? Universal in its way of knowing things and fully reflective upon itself, is not intelligence functioning in a way that transcends the limitations of matter? But if the activity transcends material limitations, must it not be proceeding from a substantial principle that correspondingly escapes dependence on matter? How could any substantial principle that was essentially limited by matter be unrestricted enough to issue into cognitive activity universal in scope? How could it reflect or bend back completely upon itself in its intellection?[19] Here the substantial principle is functioning in independence of material conditioning. To that extent it has existence in independence of matter.

Does not this mean, then, that the substantial principle of human intellection is form alone? If so, the form here possesses existence in its own right, and not just as the formal element of a material composite.[20] In itself it is a thing, incomplete of course, but able to be actual in itself and not merely in actualizing a composite. Once it is actual in itself, it is actual independently of the matter it informs. But it is actual only through its existence. Once it exists, therefore, its whole

---

[19] On the argument from universal cognition, see St. Thomas, *Summa Theologiae*, I, 75, 5c. The argument from reflection was developed by Proclus, *The Elements of Theology*, Props. 15–17; tr. E. R. Dodds (Oxford: Oxford University Press, 1933), pp. 17–21.

[20] On the difficulties in this doctrine when considered against its Aristotelian background of the soul as the form of matter, see Anton C. Pegis, "St. Thomas and the Unity of Man," in *Progress in Philosophy*, ed. James A. McWilliams (Milwaukee: The Bruce Publishing Company, 1955), pp. 153–173, and "Some Reflections on *Summa Contra Gentiles II, 56*," in *An Etienne Gilson Tribute*, ed. Charles J. O'Neil (Milwaukee: Marquette University Press, 1959), pp. 169–188.

tendency is only toward actuality, toward existence. In this respect it is conditioned by no potential principle that would allow destruction. Once it exists, consequently, it can no more be separated from the existence than from the actuality that is the form itself.[21]

From this standpoint can the existence of the substantial principle of intellectual activity be regarded as contingent? Must it not rather be termed necessarily existence? Once bestowed upon the form, it necessarily remains with it. In the case of man, the substantial form, just as in animals and plants, is traditionally called a soul. The above considerations show that the human soul, once it receives existence, is indestructible by any process of nature. Its existence is necessary. Existence is bestowed upon it in a way that places the existence above the contingent level, for it is not bestowed with any dependence upon a material element.

The question, moreover, is not quite the same as that of immortality or survival. These terms have overtones of future life. But just in itself, necessary existence or indestructibility does not guarantee life after separation of soul from matter. To do so, the reasoning would have to show how human intelligence could function naturally in independence of the images furnished it by internal sensation. The philosophical starting points, however, offer no means for establishing any other origin of human intellection than through sensation, or for showing how it could naturally function except in sensible imagery.

The necessary character of the human soul's existence, however, does show that it cannot be given existence through any process of nature, just as it cannot be destroyed through any natural process. The reason is correspondingly the same. The existence bestowed upon the soul is necessary existence, exis-

---

[21] Cf. St. Thomas, *Summa Theologiae*, I, 75, 6c; *Quaestio disputata de Anima*, 14c.

tence that is not dependent upon the capacity of a material element to acquire a new form. The existence of the soul, accordingly, is not imparted as the existence of a material composite. It is not produced by way of change in matter from one form to another. It cannot be caused in the way new material composites are continually being brought about in the cosmic processes, even though they may be processes that give life. All these processes are dependent upon a material that they fashion into a new form, and through the form they bestow new existence directly upon the composite. They confer contingent existence only.

But the existence of the human soul is necessary existence, existence that is not conferred directly upon the composite but upon the form only, existence that cannot be produced by way of a change of matter to a new form, but which has to be bestowed directly upon the soul itself. Each human soul, then, has to be given existence directly in itself, and not just as a development of something material. In a word, each human soul has to be created by a special act of efficiency on the part of subsistent existence. It cannot be produced through the mediacy of finite and noncreative causes, causes that require material upon which to work. This special creation will have to hold both for the original appearance of man in the evolutionary process, and in each instance of generative activity by which the human race continues to be procreated.

Can this in any way be called interference from the outside? How can it be so regarded, when the activity of subsistent existence in things is not at all from the outside, but profoundly from within. It attains things from the standpoint of their own existence, which is the actuality that is most intimate in them. It is the effect of a cause that is working entirely from within the cosmic processes. It is always at their core, for they are always bringing something new into existence in virtue of the concurrence of the primary efficient activity.

There is no possibility, then, of regarding the special creation of each human soul as interference with the cosmic processes from without. But is there any reason to consider it as interference at all? Rather, is it not doing just what nature calls for? Is it not activity fully in accord with the exigencies of the natural processes, instead of any kind of interference with them? When the development of organic matter reaches the point where an intellectual principle is required for it, in the course of the evolutionary surge onward toward the noosphere, do not the exigencies of nature itself insist that this principle be conferred? Do they not call for the type of activity by which this principle may be introduced into the cosmic development? But here the activity required is the special creation of each soul. Far from interference in the process, it is what the nature of the process itself demands.

Nor is there any difficulty from the standpoint of the primary efficient cause. The omnipotent and omnipresent activity of subsistent existence is by way of concurrence continually imparting existence to the activities and effects of the secondary causes. What difficulty is there for it to continue the work by genuinely creative action, when and where the nature of the activity of the secondary causes requires it? Far from interference, it is the naturally demanded continuance and completion of the activity found in the processes of nature. Surely, given a correct view of omnipotence, there is no more difficulty for it to create than to concur. Why should it not act in either way as the natures of things require? The natures are but the possibilities. The power to actualize these possibilities, in the ways respectively called for, lies in omnipotence.

There is, accordingly, no conflict whatsoever between scientific hypotheses of cosmic and organic evolution, on the one hand and, on the other, the metaphysical conclusions of creation in regard to the cosmos and each human soul. Rather, the views are complementary and support each other in genuine intellectual harmony. It is far from a case of the child's greediness for both alternatives, far from a desire both to have one's cake and to eat it. As Plato[22] showed in regard to stability and motion in the universe, so here too one is required to "say both." Both creation and concurrence, both the activity of the primary cause and the activity of the secondary causes, have their respective parts in the integral functioning of the universe. To don blinders in respect of either level of causality, whether in the wake of Marx or of Malebranche, is to shut oneself off from ever attaining a fully rounded understanding of reality.

Besides real existence in the world, cognitional existence also is bestowed upon things as they are known in the various cognitive activities. Here the existence is given them by the activity of the knower, as one can observe through reflection upon one's own cognition and conclude through analogy in regard to cognition by others. Since cognitional existence is produced by a secondary cause, will not all the requirements of concurrence on the part of the primary cause, both antecedent and simultaneous, hold at least equally in its respect? And as regards the specification of cognitional existence, does not a further though subsidiary complication arise? Real existence, since it is in the thing itself, is specified only by the thing it makes exist. The real existence of a man is entirely human, that of a horse is entirely equine. But cognitional existence is received not in the thing itself, but in the cognitive activity of the knower. It is therefore doubly specified.

It is indeed the cognitional existence of the thing known, but it is also a different kind of cognitional existence insofar as it is known through intellection or sensation, through sight

---

[22] *Sophist,* 249D. On the translation "we must say, like children in their wishes, 'Both,' " see Lewis Campbell, *The Sophistes and Politicus of Plato* (Oxford, 1867), p. 131, n. 10. Whatever further allusion may lie behind the Greek text, is it too much to say that a little experiment will elicit the same type of answer from children anywhere?

or hearing or imagination. The type of cognitive activity clearly enters into the specification of the cognitional existence achieved in it. The difference between real and cognitional existence, accordingly, arises not from the side of existence but from the side of the natures involved. Of itself existence still manifests no principle of diversification. Even the basic difference between real and cognitional existence arises from a further nature, namely the nature of the cognitive activity in which cognitional existence takes place.

The bestowal of existence, consequently, can be studied in fairly extensive detail on the basis of what is known through judgment, and through reasoning about the ways in which existence has to be specified by other natures and arise as something new. True, in all this procedure there is no understanding from the inside. One never penetrates the nature of existence in the way one understands the nature of a triangle. One has no concept of it that would furnish a ground for distinguishing between real and cognitional existence, subsistent existence and imparted existence. As far as the concept goes, these are all just existence, to be further specified not by anything in the line of existence but by natures that are other than existence. Yet on the basis of what one knows in these roundabout ways, one is able to conclude that the original bestowal of existence upon finite things was through creation and that in regard to each human soul it still is.

Once given, existence just as necessarily has to be conserved by the activity of its efficient cause. In the universe finite agents as secondary causes bestow existence on other things, always under the mediate or immediate antecedent concurrence of the primary cause, and always with its immediate simultaneous concurrence. In these ways the experienced or presumed activity of the secondary cause is safeguarded, while the concurrent activity of the infinite primary cause accounts for the radically new existence that is thereby bestowed.

CHAPTER VI

Meaning of Existence

What, then, is the overall bearing of the multifaceted and deeply penetrating considerations that have been assembled in the preceding chapters? Has not their scope become surprisingly far-reaching? Does not the mini-sentence, "It is" or "It exists," turn out to be a means of conveying extremely pertinent and widely ranging information, when it is probed to the fullness of its own intrinsic content and the requirements to which it gives witness? Even the least actuality of existence in the observable world leads the mind to subsistent existence as present and intimately active everywhere. Should reference to the ordinary workaday and tarnished existence as *ens vulgare*[1] be allowed to blind one's intuition of its richness, or prompt one to seek a more exotic starting point for the science of metaphysics? Just as the assertion, "It is green," is able to unfold in all the superior predicates of the category of quality under the scrutiny of the trained intellect, so the mini-sentence, "It is," can spark a philosophical procedure that leads to the most sublime and relevant truths attainable by unaided human reason.

---

[1] See Thomas C. O'Brien, "Book Reviews," *The New Scholasticism*, XXXVIII (1964), 272.

Any existence whatsoever, when accepted as known through assertion and interpreted in the way that has been sketched in the foregoing chapters, is enough to establish subsistent existence. In the mini-sentence, however, the "it" presumably is not meant to refer to subsistent existence, which just in itself furnishes no ground for distinction between itself and its existential actuality. As an initial assertion, the mini-sentence hardly could be expected to refer meaningfully to subsistent being, without explicit indication that it was being offered as the conclusion of a long and intricate demonstration. But if in the mind of its proponent the "it" in the mini-sentence was in fact meant to refer to subsistent existence as the subject of the assertion, the problem how subject and existential actuality were being distinguished would immediately arise and lead to the consideration of something finite, for instance the man making the assertion, as the basis for differentiating thing from existence.

The way, accordingly, would be open at once for the study of finite being. On the other hand, if the mini-sentence, as may be presumed, refers directly to some finite thing, the question of the distinction between the "it" and the "is" will immediately arise. When what the "is" expresses is found to be the object of judgment, and prior and accidental to the thing expressed by the "it," the data are informative and dynamic enough to spark the cogent though difficult demonstration that reaches subsistent existence and its ever present efficient causality throughout the universe.

This of course, is the situation when existence is assessed as an object originally known through judgment. But apart from St. Thomas Aquinas, how often in the whole history of Western philosophy has existence been so assessed and followed through to its astonishing entailments?[2] Have not other

<hr/>

[2] The genealogical entry, "Thomas genuit Gilson," in L.-M. Régis, "Gilson's Being and Some Philosophers," The Modern Schoolman, XXVIII (1951), 125, gives terse but eloquent expression to the long lacuna. Reprinted in

ways of interpreting it become so deeply ingrained in our tradition that the Thomistic texts have hardly a chance of making their message clear? Indeed the texts themselves have been habitually engrafted on other stocks and compelled to live a life alien to their own. Western philosophical tradition, beyond doubt, always has been radically pluralistic. Yet it is cultivated as a single garden, in which survival depends upon the emergence and the propagation of the fittest characteristics. Extreme care, therefore, has to be exercised in the cross-fertilization. The main stock has to be safeguarded, even while one is making full use of the best in other strains.

So, alien though the other ways of thinking may be to a metaphysics based on existence known through judgment, they all are parts of Western philosophical enterprise. They form the general matrix in which any thoroughgoing interpretation of existence is to be undertaken today. They spring authentically from Western ways of approaching reality on the philosophic level, and bring out myriad aspects of the problem that one cannot afford to neglect. Each has its message to convey. Each has to be listened to carefully in seeing an answer to Heidegger's question "How does it stand with being?"[3]

At the very beginning of the Western encounter with being as a distinct object of thought, Parmenides had regarded it as a form and had watched it absorb everything else into itself at the level on which reason functioned. Only on the lower level of appearance did the multiplicity and the process of a cosmos remain. Does not the message ring clearly? Isolate the aspect of being that is seen in things around you, project it immediately as a nature, and what happens? You find that it has drawn into its own unity all the things in which it is found. Plurality in things and change in things become unintelligible.

Gilson, *Being and Some Philosophers*, 2nd ed. (Toronto: The Pontifical Institute of Mediaeval Studies, 1952), p. 221.

[3] Martin Heidegger, *An Introduction to Metaphysics*, tr. Ralph Manheim (New Haven: Yale University Press, 1959), p. 32.

The all-absorbing character of being came into Western thought with Parmenides, and it came to stay. Its shock was rude, and had to be resisted at all costs. The easygoing process philosophies of Ionia were compelled to freeze the notion of being into a fixed plurality of Empedoclean elements or the unlimited number of shapes in the Democritean atoms. The expansive force of the notion was artificially restrained within these basic formal limits. In Plato, with much greater sympathy for the notion's reach, true being was located in a world of separate forms. Each of these was a distinct nature in itself, with being as but one form among the others though shared by them all.

The compromise of participation strove valiantly to stay the onslaught of absorption, and left its powerful impact enduringly enough on subsequent thought. But soon the difficulties in separating the natures of things from their sensible instances and an original concentration on the actuality of form, led Aristotle to conclude that pure actuality was to be found in a multiplicity of separate forms different in nature from those of the sensible world, with the general notion of being no longer regarded as something real but relegated to the status of merely a concept in the human mind.[4] In this framework no possibility of reasoning to any infinite and necessarily unique being remained open. There was no way of establishing being as a real all-inclusive nature. Yet the emphasis placed by the Stagirite on the character of actuality in form and being was destined to bear significant fruit in a later stage of the evolutionary mutations.

Could the artificial restraining of being to the confines of each particular form, the deliberate preventing of its overflow

---

[4] For Aristotle, *Metaphysics*, Z 16,1040b23, nothing that is shared commonly can be the substance of a thing. This is applied to the notion of being, *ibid.*, b16–27. On the problem, see my comments in *The Doctrine of Being in the Aristotelian Metaphysics*, 2nd ed. (Toronto: The Pontifical Institute of Mediaeval Studies, 1963), pp. 456, 471–472.

in reality from one form to another, be expected to prevail indefinitely against the inborn tendency of the notion toward unity and all-inclusiveness? Aristotle, while striving hard to establish being as a single genus that could be dealt with by a single science, seems to acquiesce in an inevitable plurality as its primary instance.[5] Plotinus, instead of allowing the desired oneness to follow upon being, located it as a principle prior to being. In this way he could keep being as a plurality of forms and restrict intelligence to knowledge of these forms. But the first principle of all was thereby placed above being and rendered attainable only in a manner superior to intelligence. Patristic tradition, identifying the God of scriptural revelation with being,[6] did not hesitate in the philosophical setting of Neoplatonism to regard the first principle of all things as located in this way beyond the grasp of unaided human intellection. Being, accordingly, was placed above intelligible form. But the Christian doctrine of creation, interpreted against the Neoplatonic background, meant that the first effect in creatures was being.[7] With nature defined in this framework as whatever can be grasped in any way by the intellect and, accordingly, restricted to what is known through the thing's essence or definition,[8] the stage was set for a meaningful distinction between being and essence, and for an original

---

[5] See ibid., p. 14.

[6] On the patristic texts, see Cornelia J. De Vogel, " 'Ego sum qui sum' et sa signification pour une philosophie chrétienne." Revue des Sciences Religieuses, XXXV (1961), 346–354.

[7] See Liber de Causis, Prop. 4. The reason why being is the first is immediately given: "This is because being is above sensation and above soul and above intelligence, and after the first cause nothing is wider than it or caused in priority to it." Ibid. A concise use of the tenet may be seen in St. Thomas, In I Sententiarum, d. 8, q. 1, a. 3, Contra; ed. Mandonnet, I, 199, and at Summa Contra Gentiles, II, 21, Adhuc effectus. Cf.: "Now the first among all effects is being; for all else are certain determinations of it." Summa Contra Gentiles, III, 66, Item.

[8] See the understanding of the Boethian definition in St. Thomas, De Ente et Essentia, c. I; ed. Roland-Gosselin, p. 4.5–9. Cf. William of Auvergne, De Trin., c. II; ed. Paris, 1674, Suppl. p. 2b.

way of knowing being that differed radically from the way of knowing nature or thing.

This development is found in point of historical fact in St. Thomas Aquinas. The tenet that the being of a thing is originally grasped through judgment and not through conceptualization seems introduced in the theological method of St. Thomas as the necessary epistemological support for an already accepted notion of God. If such be the case, it is entirely possible that St. Thomas was led to his metaphysical starting point by meditating on a scriptural notion of God, interpreted against a Neoplatonic background. It may be the case, likewise, that to appreciate the philosophical force and understand the full metaphysical significance of this tenet, the easiest way — perhaps, one might insist, the psychologically indicated way — is to retrace the steps by which it emerged out of its original historic setting at a definite epoch of Christian theology. It also may be possible to take the stand that other thinkers have missed this apparently obvious starting point because they did not use the theological approach.[9] But with all this stated and weighed, the simple fact remains that the tenet is presented by St. Thomas as something immediately observable. Not the slightest indication is given that it is meant as a conclusion from other premises, or that any religious authority is being appealed to for its acceptance. Where in Scripture or in previous theological tradition or in the beliefs of the faithful is there any hint of the notion that existence is grasped through judgment only, instead of through conceptualization? The formulation of the question makes it appear too absurd to require any further pursuit of an answer. No, the tenet is presented clearly as something open to unaided intellectual scrutiny. As the starting point for metaphysical reasoning it stands or falls on its own intrinsic evidence. For use in a metaphysical

---

[9] On this possibility, see E. Gilson, *Elements of Christian Philosophy* (New York: Doubleday, 1960), pp. 131–133.

context, accordingly, it can rest on nothing other than what one experiences in one's own encounter with the things in the observable universe.

However, in a way that is still far from clear historically, this truly remarkable insight of St. Thomas did not have any recorded influence on the thinking of his own or the immediately following epochs. Some two years after his death, the centuries-long discussions on the distinction between essence and existence broke out.[10] In the Christian doctrine of creation existence was something that was given the creature, not something that had its origin in the creature's nature. Against this Christian background being for Aquinas was existence and existence was being. But the more remote Greek philosophical background did not allow itself to be easily transcended. For it form was being, nature was being. As a result two types of being sprang up in these discussions. One was existential being (*esse existentiae*). The other was essential being (*esse essentiae*). The problem at issue was how the two were to be distinguished. A distinction between existence and being could now be excogitated, since there was a type of being, namely essential being, that could be contrasted with existence.

Worse still, the two alleged types of being, essential being and existential being, became contrasted with each other as two different things (res) or realities. The existence of things, accordingly, was projected as though it itself were another reality or thing. In this setting, no matter what care was taken to avoid the absurdity, a thing's existence could hardly escape being presented as one more reality alongside the other realities in the thing and, accordingly, as a reality existent itself.[11]

---

[10] On these see P. Mandonnet, "Les premières disputes sur la distinction réelle entre l'essence et l'existence, 1276–1287," *Revue Thomiste*, XVIII (1910), 741–765; J. Paulus, "Les disputes d'Henri de Gand et de Gilles de Rome sur la Distinction de l'essence et de l'existence," *Archives d'Histoire Littéraire et Doctrinale du Moyen Age*, XVII (1942), 323–358.

[11] Cf.: ". . . *ita ut ipsum individuum ex duabus realitatibus in rerum natura existentibus . . . , essentia et existentia, coalescat*" (". . . so that the

In it the functions of thing and being became in this way identified, even ironically, in the explicit effort to keep them sharply distinct. But the consequence, from the viewpoint of basic metaphysical considerations, was even more lethal. With existence assessed as a reality itself instead of as the actuality of *all* the reality present, no reason could emerge for seeking a nonconceptual origin for human knowledge of it. Existence could not help but be regarded as apprehended originally through a concept. Then the troubles started. Subsequent philosophy scrutinized the concept carefully, found in it no characteristic content, equated it with the concept of nothing, and eliminated from the realm of intelligibility the discipline for which it set up the subject matter, metaphysics.[12] Against this background could a sorrier picture be imagined for an answer to Heidegger's question about how the case stands with being?

The existentialist reaction, from Kierkegaard on, was drastic. As confined to the limiting objectivity of conceptual knowledge, being left no room for freedom and the characteristically human dimension. The obvious and compelling drama in the role of existence as a vibrant actuality that surges above the inhibitions of form and breaks loose into exhilarating and unpredictable worlds of novelty, was seized upon with avidity. It was lived exuberantly by an avant-garde generation. In a setting of concern, anxiety, nausea, and despair, the freedom that is existence drove a powerful salient into the staid lines of conventional European philosophy.

In the slowly moving and much more cautious American philosophical circles it attracted interest enough but compara-

---

individual itself coalesces from two realities existing in the real world, existence and essence"). J. Gredt, *Elementa Philosophiae Aristotelico-Thomisticae*, 7th ed. (Freiburg i. Breisgau, 1937), II, 105 (no. 704, 2).

[12] See André Marc, *L'Idée de l'Être chez St. Thomas et dans la Scolastique Postérieure* (Paris, 1933); E. Gilson, *Being and Some Philosophers*, 2nd ed. (Toronto: The Pontifical Institute of Mediaeval Studies, 1952), pp. 74–142; N. R. Hanson, "On the Impossibility of Any Future Metaphysics," *Philosophical Studies*, XI (1960), 86–96; Robert T. Sandin, "The Concept of Reality and the Elimination of Metaphysics," *The Monist*, L (1966), 87–97.

tively little genuine adhesion, despite its prominent advocates. In theology and religion, however, it has raged everywhere like wildfire. True, even to express itself as a philosophy it had to temper its subjectivity with objective structures, and its inherent need to do so did not pass unnoticed.[13] Its close association with phenomenology has allowed it to adopt in practice an eidetic framework.[14] Quite possibly its death knell has been sounded by the current pulls from wide ranging tendencies toward a general matrix of structuralism,[15] as concrete thought continues "to compel phenomenology to rethink itself"[16] and "formalism" both as a term and a notion begins to gain philosophical respectability. Be this as it may, the impact of ex-

---

[13] E.g.: "For existentialism in purity cannot exist because it needs universals — essences — to make statements at all, even about existence. . . . Only in confrontation with the essential structures of being can existentialism speak." Paul Tillich, "Relation of Metaphysics and Theology," Review of Metaphysics, X (1956), 63.

[14] ". . . how could it happen that in France the two movements became practically synonymous? . . . the view became almost inevitable that Heidegger's existential philosophy represented the logical development and fulfillment of the original Phenomenological Movement." Herbert Spiegelberg, The Phenomenological Movement (The Hague: Martinus Nijhoff, 1960), II, 410. Cf. pp. 415–420.

[15] "More specifically, around 1962, structuralism, from a working method known to and practiced by specialists, became a fashionable philosophy discussed in as many circles as Sartre's existentialism had been after world war II; . . ." Jacques Ehrmann, "Introduction," Yale French Studies, XXXVI–XXXVII (1966), p. 6. On the notion of "a structure," see ibid., p. 7; cf.: "les structures connaissables émergent d'abord du domaine des formes sur lesquelles a prise l'activité humaine; mais elles tombent ensuite dans le domaine des analyses vérifiantes de la science" ("The knowable structures emerge at first from the domain of forms over which human activity has its hold; but they fall afterwards into the domain of the verifying analyses of science"). N. Mouloud, "La logiques des structures et l'epistémologie," Revue Internationale de Philosophie, XIX (1965), 333–334. On the present trend as moving from "defunct existentialism" towards structuralism, see Charles Moeller, "The Renewal of the Doctrine of Man," to be published in the Proceedings of the Congress on the Theology of the Renewal of the Church, held at Toronto, August 20–25, 1967. Others, however, see no incompatibility with existentialism in the radically human character of structuralism, based as it is on conscience and experience.

[16] Enzo Paci, "Il senso delle strutture in Lévi-Strauss," Revue Internationale de Philosophie, XIX (1965), 301. For a description of "this new kind of formalism," see Jacques Ehrmann, loc. cit., p. 6. Cf. titles listed, ibid., pp. 269–270.

istentialism has left reopened to Western thought, permanently may we hope, a door that never should have been closed to it.[17] The radical identity of freedom and existence, together with the metaphysical priority of existence over nature, should never again be omitted from the answer to the question, "How does it stand with being?"

In Britain a strongly developed approach from starting points in the realm of logic seemed to serve as effective insulation against existentialist growths, giving rise to the notion of "The English Channel, a Philosophical Chasm."[18] Propositions were accepted as starting points. Their truth values were regarded as primitive considerations. In this setting propositions are encountered that are sometimes true. Accordingly, it is possible for them to be true, in contradistinction to propositions that are accepted as always true. The possibility implies occurrences that may be called existential: "It will be out of this notion of *sometimes*, which is the same as the notion of *possible*, that we get the notion of existence."[19] Existence, accordingly, turns out to be a derivative notion, built upon a thoroughly conceptual basis. In the procedure in which propositions are generalized to a greater or lesser extent under the symbolic form of a propositional function it comes to be regarded as "essentially a property of a propositional function."[20] But in this role it quickly engendered apparently insuperable difficulties as a logical predicate.[21] At least, the discussions on the topic brought out forcefully the point that existence as a

---

[17] A lethargic tendency of the intellect to remain within the neatly definable will, of course, continue to exert its influence: "Reason dislikes the undefinable, and because pure existence is undefinable, philosophy does all it can to avoid it." E. Gilson, *The Christian Philosophy of St. Thomas Aquinas*, tr. L. K. Shook (New York: Random House, 1956), p. 44.

[18] Title of a paper by Robert Schmidt, reported in "The Secretary's Chronicle," *The New Scholasticism*, XXXIX (1965), 352.

[19] Bertrand Russell, "The Philosophy of Logical Atomism," *The Monist*, XXIX (1919), 195.

[20] *Ibid.* Cf. Chapter III, n. 6.

[21] See Chapter I, nn. 1–5 and 8.

predicate could not be assessed by the same norms as other predicates.[22] That point in itself is a notable gain, and a lasting contribution toward an answer to the question how the situation stands with being.

With the point registered as an important philosophical acquisition, however, further difficulties inherent in the conception of existence as the value of a bound variable may not be easily sidestepped. How can this approach allow for different kinds or degrees of existence?[23] Does it not restrict existence to a univocally conceived relation between propositional function and instances? What way can it open up for understanding existence as determined in different fashions by the different essences, substantial and accidental? Yet, as the encounter with existentialism clearly showed, existence has to be expressed by means of essence.[24] Any diversification or variety in it can be accounted for only in terms of essence. Without specification by the polychrome of the myriad cosmic natures, the existence mirrored in propositions can be projected only as a colorless hyaline. No new sound would ever be able to change the alleged "Eleatic monotone." No possibility would be offered for according genuine existential rights to both real and cognitional being.

Is not this last consideration of the utmost importance for the role of existence from the viewpoint of human destiny? In his real existence, a man is limited to the confines of one existent among millions. In real being he is his own physical self and nothing else. But in cognitional being his range is

---

[22] ". . . Hume is certainly right in thinking that I cannot represent the existence of non-existence of the thing by adding to my picture in an exactly parallel way to the way in which I represent the yellowness or non-yellowness of the thing by adding to the picture." Jerome Shaffer, "Existence, Predication, and the Ontological Argument," *Mind*, LXXI (1962), 317.

[23] See Chapter II, n. 26.

[24] See n. 13 of this chapter. Cf.: "Now being insofar as it is being cannot be diverse; but it can be diversified by something that is additional to being, as the being of a stone is other than the being of a man." St. Thomas, *Summa Contra Gentiles*, II, 52, Si enim.

unlimited. He can become one thing after another without cease. As the noosphere evolves and spreads he pushes his cognitional existence to the innermost recesses of the atom and to the outermost edge of the disappearing galaxies. He flings this existence unrelentingly into ever broadening worlds of literature, art, science, philosophy, theology. In cognitional existence he is able to identify himself with every possible object. He is able to keep increasing and expanding indefinitely. Cognitionally, the existence of everything that comes within his intellectual vision is his own enlarged existence.

In this way and in the volitional activity that follows upon and accompanies intellection, he is continually becoming himself and ennobling himself. Nothing will ultimately satisfy him except existence without limits, the direct union in cognitional existence with infinite being.[25] In existence only can this union be achieved, for in essence man inevitably remains finite. Further all-important precisions and qualifications are necessary, but at least from the viewpoint of philosophy existence does appear to hold in its meaning the spiritual destiny of mankind.

In this existential setting the full meaning of Aristotle's intuitions become clear. The Stagirite had observed in his own reflective experience that "mind is in a sense potentially whatever is thinkable, though actually it is nothing until it has

---

[25] Cf.: "Now, this should be observed as obtaining in the same way in the order of intelligible being as it does in substantial or physical being. . . . So, it is manifest that the divine essence may be related to the created intellect as an intelligible species by which it understands, . . . This immediate vision of God is promised us in Scripture: . . ." St. Thomas, *Summa Contra Gentiles*, III, 51; tr. Vernon J. Bourke. On the natural desire for this ultimate goal, see *ibid.*, III, 25. On its inclusion of "the full sufficiency of all the goods . . . required for happiness," see *ibid.*, III, 63. On the perpetuity that is necessary for it, see *ibid.*, III, 48 and 62; and, in contrast, from an existentialist viewpoint: "What I rejected, with all my heart and soul, was the horror of that endless night, which, since it did not exist, would never *be* horrible, but held infinite horror for me, who *did* exist." Simone de Beauvoir, *The Prime of Life*, tr. Peter Green (Cleveland and New York: World Publishing Company, 1962), p. 475.

thought."[26] He had seen that "actual knowledge is identical with its object,"[27] and that, accordingly, "The soul is in a way all existing things."[28] But what is the "in a sense" or "in a way" that allows two different things to *be* one, while each retains its own identity as subject and as object, respectively? How is it that the mind *is* whatever is thinkable, that the soul *is* all things? In Aristotle there is no existential penetration into the problem. The fact is merely noted and stated with care. To explain it metaphysically, the painstaking elaboration of the distinctions between nature and existence, and between the real and cognitional existence of the same thing, becomes indispensable. Is not this elaboration equally necessary to understand the restatement of the ancient Aristotelian intuition in a modern context: ". . . to *be* more is in the first place to *know* more,"[29] that "*to see or to perish* is the very condition laid upon everything that makes up the universe,"[30] and that, in a context in which "blessed" traditionally expresses the ultimate destiny of man, "it is so vital and so blessed to *know*"?[31]

Is not the searching existential penetration necessary in order to make these assertions intelligible? And, under existential explanation, does not the whole picture of human existence and human destiny begin to make sense? Does it not show clearly, on the metaphysical level, how the meaning of existence holds the destiny not only of the West but of all mankind? If in fact intellectual contemplation is the supreme goal of all human striving, as the *Nicomachean Ethics* so

---

[26] *De Anima*, III 4,429b30–31; Oxford tr.

[27] *Ibid.*, III 7,431a1–2; Oxford tr.

[28] *Ibid.*, III 8,431b21; Oxford tr.

[29] Teilhard de Chardin, *The Future of Man*, tr. Norman Denny (New York and Evanston: Harper & Row, 1964), p. 19. However, although Teilhard (p. 126) claims that "as we draw near to the Whole, physics, metaphysics and religion strangely converge," the existential interpretation of knowledge as found in Aquinas leaves completely intact the specific objects and differences of the sciences.

[30] Teilhard de Chardin, *The Phenomenon of Man*, tr. Bernard Wall (New York and Evanston: Harper & Row, 1959), p. 31.

[31] *Ibid.*

tellingly demonstrates, is not an existential understanding of
this supremely active and in every way satisfying destiny necessary in order to do full justice to both the Dionysian and the
Apollonian aspirations of man?

But to achieve so enviable an understanding of the supreme
questions in human life, the concepts and techniques of nearly
twenty-five centuries of traditional Western thought have to
be mastered. There is no other way. It is a hard way, it is a
long way, yet its demand is imperative. There is no question of
using the uninteresting and lifeless copies that clog school
manuals and provide ample cannon fodder for hostile diatribes.
One has to go directly to the concentrated life in the genuine
sculpture,

> The stone that breathes and struggles,
> The brass that seems to speak; —
> Such cunning they who dwell on high
> Have given unto the Greek.[32]

The forging of the Western philosophical techniques and
concepts undoubtedly began with the Greeks and progressed
surprisingly far with them. But it did not end with them. The
Promethean fire continued throughout the Patristic and Scholastic periods to keep the bronze malleable, as further concepts such as person, essence, existence, subsistence, creation,
omnipotence, and many others were slowly and painfully ham-
mered into vitally expressive shape. The skill or technical
"cunning" required for apt philosophical confrontation with
new problems did not desert Western man after the close of
the Greek era. It remained creatively alive through medieval
into modern times. But while medieval minds treasured the
Greek and Patristic achievements even in revitalizing the old
and creating the new, the modern mentality has tended to
neglect the inspiring techniques so skillfully and painstakingly
worked out in the encounters of the past. It fails to take seriously enough the vibrant intellectuality that pulsates through

[32] Macaulay, The Prophecy of Capys, 28 (in the Lays of Ancient Rome).

> The many-colored tablets bright
> With loves and wars of old.[33]

Certainly in regard to the two basic metaphysical problems for human destiny the results have not been encouraging. No new substitutes in philosophical technique have been devised in recent times to show that being subsists and that the intellectual principle in each individual man possesses necessary existence. Is it not quite generally accepted today that the existence of God cannot be demonstrated by unaided human reason?[34] How many will allow demonstrative force to a philosophical procedure that would establish the indestructibility of the human soul?[35] Yet are not these the utterly fundamental tenets that a Christian philosophy seeks to make secure for a believer in search of understanding? Nor does the profoundly intimate efficient causality of the primary cause throughout every finite thing and every finite activity, with its far-reaching consequences for understanding the traditional Christian teaching on prayer of petition and on reward and punishment, fare any better in ways of thinking that deliberately discard the carefully forged techniques of the past. With the present-day

---

[33] *Ibid.*

[34] E.g.: "Religious people have, in fact, come to acquiesce, in the total absence of any cogent proofs of the Being they believe in; they even find it positively satisfying that something so far surpassing clear conception should also surpass the possibility of demonstration." J. N. Findlay, "Can God's Existence Be Disproved," *Mind*, LVII (1948), 176. The proofs are accordingly but "fallacious existential trimmings" for the religious spirit; *ibid.*, p. 183. Or, while conceding the difficulty in exposing any sophism in the demonstration, one may content oneself with the observation that the proofs are ineffectual for convincing an unbeliever, and for a believer are useless or in their very idea "a slur on what is for him a sacred evidence" — Gabriel Marcel, *The Mystery of Being*, tr. René Hague (London, 1951), II, 176; cf. p. 174. Finally, the problem may be regarded as an open philosophical question, without bearing on faith: "The possibility of proving God's existence is a philosophical problem and weighty thinkers are ranged on both sides of the question." E. Fontinell, "Postscript," in *Speaking of God*, ed. Denis Dirscherl (Milwaukee: The Bruce Publishing Company, 1967), p. 158.

[35] Even the Thomistic tradition has not been firm on this tenet; in regard to the difficulties that come to the fore with Cajetan, see E. Gilson, "Autour de Pomponazzi," *Archives d'Histoire Doctrinale et Littéraire du Moyen Age*, XXVIII (1961), 173–183; 275–277.

reading public, of course, anyone is free to cast aspersion on these Scholastic techniques. But what no one can do is to point out any other satisfactory developments that might replace them for the work they were intended to do.

In this respect the whole accomplishment of the past has to be brought to bear upon current problems. It cannot be dismembered or truncated if it is to function in vital fashion. Concepts have to be clarified and deepened, but not discarded once they have earned their place in the living tradition. The ten Aristotelian categories, the predicables, the distinctions of conceptualization and judgment and reasoning, the notions of actuality and potentiality, of essence and existence, of the four causes, of the transcendental properties, of necessity and contingency and freedom, of speculative and practical science, are all required. They are integral parts of the living philosophic tradition that breathes and struggles and speaks through the carefully sculptured and vitally palpitating formulae. To start cutting, for instance, by discarding the categories of position and of state, may seem innocent enough. But it can hardly help having repercussions within the integral structure, initiating a process that keeps rejecting more and more of the organism and eventually deprives it of life. Does not the situation correspond to that faced in a religious context by Browning's bishop?

> I cut and cut again!
> First cut the Liquefaction, what comes last
> But Fichte's clever cut at God himself?
> (*Bishop Blougram's Apology*, 742–744)

To drop the more complex categories, such as position and state, out of a laudable motive of simplification, can hardly help bring into question the status of the relations upon which these categories are founded, and may quite easily jeopardize the reality that was accredited to relations in the full bloom of Scholastic thought. One may polish these concepts, explain the different senses in which they are categories, and their own characteristic bearing upon the course of philosophical thinking. But to discard them outright is to open the door for trouble. To disregard the development of judgment as the original intuition of being, and still try to use Scholasticism to face genuinely existential problems, is to court the tragedy that Neoscholasticism has experienced during the past one hundred years.

To look upon the proof for the existence of God from motion as the Aristotelian demonstration of separate substance, neglecting thereby the existential development given to its key notion of actuality by Thomas Aquinas during the middle ages, is to advance an argument that cannot stand up under any serious critique.[36] To expect the arguments of the *Phaedo* to establish the indestructibility of the human soul while taking no account of the necessary existence required by a subsistent form, is to leave them open to rather easy rebuttal, or at least to allow them to remain quite inconclusive. Concepts like essence and existence, necessity or contingency, have to be chiseled painfully into shape. All being has to be carefully eliminated from the notion of essence, and the limiting factor of essence has to be kept out of the concept of existence. Necessity and contingency have to be developed in a way that will account for freedom. But these are problems of polishing and purifying, and not of discarding what is already there.

With the techniques that have gradually taken shape throughout the long course of traditional philosophy, then, one has the means of working out a thoroughgoing interpretation of existence. Existence turns out, under their spectroscopy, to be far more than a mere word with only a haze for its meaning. In its spectra can be read truths that affect human destiny on levels more enduring than that on which the galaxies recede

---

[36] On this topic, see my articles, "Aquinas and the Proof from the 'Physics,'" *Mediaeval Studies*, XXVIII (1966), 119–150; "Actuality in the 'Prima Via' of St. Thomas," *ibid.*, XXIX (1967), 26–46.

and the elementary particles run their course. In requiring cogently that existence subsist in itself as the primary and ever-present efficient cause of all finite things, the existential starting point enables a man to acquire a profound understanding of the principle in which his being and life and activity are located.[37] In showing that the existence of the human soul is necessary, not contingent, the existential reasoning allows for vision of a goal beyond the merely material and dissoluble. In understanding cognition as genuinely new existence, it explains how man can keep becoming himself through all the arts and sciences of the noosphere, and yet remain open to a far more sublime destiny of an existence that consists in direct knowledge of infinite being.

Metaphysics, of course, cannot be expected to provide the type of knowledge that puts a man in immediate possession of infinite being, even less than it could be expected to furnish the experimental and mathematical knowledge that makes man master over nature. Just as its universal sweep leaves full play for the particular sciences in their own spheres,[38] so does it allow ample and more than ample room for the activities of faith and sacred theology. What it does is to establish a strong though sufficiently pliable framework in which these can spark and guide an authentically intellectual life. Intellectually certain that all finite existence is being produced by subsistent being, a man is protected against any temptation to fear that he might be creating God after his own image and likeness. Sure on demonstrable reasoning that he is actuated by necessary and not contingent existence in the intellectual side of his nature, he is not at all surprised at the invitation of the

---

[37] Cf. Chapter V, n. 15.
[38] Cf.: ". . . metaphysics which treats of all things insofar as they are beings, not descending to the distinctive cognition of the moral or natural realms." St. Thomas, *In I Sententiarum*, Prol., q. 1, a. 2, Solut.; ed. Mandonnet, I, 10. "But from the common principles of being insofar as it is being, adequate causal understanding is not had of something that exists in particular fashion." *In IV Metaphysicorum*, lect. 2, Cathala no. 559.

Gospels to live for a kingdom that is not of this world. Knowing that the culmination of his existence and destiny and freedom is the intellectual possession of the highest possible object, he is not the least abashed in learning through faith that the supreme goal of all his living and striving is to see God face to face for all eternity.[39] Likewise secure in his estimate of any knowledge as cognitional existence, he is able to see all scientific and artistic achievements fit harmoniously into a unified picture and to rejoice in a munificence able to provide him constantly with the cultural supports that he needs in his journey toward his one ultimate destiny.

In all these ways, then, does not the meaning of existence spread itself incisively throughout the most important questions of human life? In its all-pervading actuality does it not, on the metaphysical level, make manifest the radiant destiny of mankind? But to cause awareness of this function in practical life, does it not have to be approached, frankly, in the light of the philosophical techniques that have been progressively developed through the long centuries of traditional Western thought? With the aid of these techniques a profound and widely creative philosophy of existence is able to emerge. Can anyone really afford to neglect these tenets of the past, or discard them or disdain them as aberrations of less advanced ages than our own? Would not that attitude be witness to a temporal chauvinism that has no more right to any place in a

---

[39] From the very beginning of his teaching career, St. Thomas made himself clear on the status of Aristotelian contemplation as belonging to the present life: ". . . all who have thought correctly have placed the contemplation of God as the goal of human life. Now the contemplation of God is twofold. One way is through creatures. This way is imperfect, for the reason just given. In this contemplation the Philosopher, in the tenth book of the *Ethics*, placed contemplative happiness. Yet this is wayfaring happiness (*felicitas viae*); and to it is directed the whole of philosophical knowledge, which stems from what is knowable in creatures." *In I Sententiarum*, Prol., q. 1, a. 1, Solut.; I, 7–8.

On the metaphor of the wayfarer (*homo viator*) and its history through medieval times, see Gerhart B. Ladner, "Homo Viator: Mediaeval Ideas on Alienation and Order," *Speculum*, XLII (1967), 233–259.

well-balanced culture than has racial snobbery or political jingoism? Would it not be running the risk of a break with the life-giving sources of the ongoing Western philosophical endeavor?

On the other hand, philosophy cannot be repetition. It has to be always creative, or else it will not be genuine. But unlike divine creation, it is not creation out of nothing. It is creative evolution, the continuing of a development process, the growth of insights that have been slowly and painfully engendered in the past. Only in the throes of actual life-giving may these achievements of the past continue their vital functioning. Not as stereotyped and cheapened in pale replicas, but as breathing and struggling in their original vibrant settings, can these techniques be of real service today. Far from dispensing with the gains of modern thinking, they clamor for common incorporation of all into the one pulsating bloodstream of Western thought. They need the conceptual clarifications promoted by Hume and the linguistic analysts and by the Nominalists of all ages, the lucidity of Descartes, the penetrating scrutiny of Kant, the wide-ranging sweep of Idealistic thought, the exacting discipline of the modern logics, the primacy accorded to existence and the vivid role given to existentials in the thought currents of the present century, and the poise of the eidetic or the formal in phenomenology and structuralism.

All these gains contribute their worth and their welcome help in vivifying as well as expanding the use of traditional philosophic techniques. They should keep fanning them into continued and progressively brighter glow. Genus, species, and individual, actuality and potentiality, existence and essence, substance and the nine accidents, the four causes, the speculative and the practical, and the other basic concepts of traditional philosophy, need the incessant development and the relevant animation of each new age. Even though the most satisfactory approach to existence may turn out to be the

metaphysical truths elaborated by St. Thomas Aquinas, these
truths found in his works have not only to be read against
their own historical background but also to be kept alive in
all the current pluralistic setting of contemporary thought.
A Thomism that is "narrowly Thomistic" cannot hope to be
a genuine Thomism.

Just as the radical pluralism of both Greek and medieval
philosophy was able to generate and maintain a common vital
tradition of philosophic thought, is there any reason apparent
why all that is worthwhile in modern thinking cannot continue
to be absorbed authentically into the common life stream of
the Western philosophic enterprise? Is it necessary to regard
the newer insights as but brilliantly colored autumn leaves,
testifying to previous life but now irrevocably detached from
the parent trunk on which they grew?[40] Why may they not
be integrated? Why can they not form part of a common life
stream? Does not the full-fledged life of Western thought
require the exacting disciplines of analysis? Does it not equally
require the play of poignant existentials? No matter how rationally certain one is of the metaphysical truths concerning God
and the soul, and no matter how logically cogent one makes
the form of the demonstrations, one has still to face continually
in daily life the situations that give rise to anxiety, dread, joy,
and triumph, with the full responsibility for the outcome of
one's actions. The dimension of freedom and consequent responsibility keeps bringing ever new encounters with life's
agonizing or victorious phases, in all their concern and ab-
surdities and nausea and fear and delights. Throughout this
welter of existence, moreover, does not Western thought require also the sobering control of essence, deepened as the

40 E.g.: ". . . even the best of existential writing . . . is a floating philosophy
— vivid as autumn leaves, but as incapable as they of taking hold again of a
parent branch. In this it is neither better nor worse than the analytic
philosophy in vogue elsewhere." Marjorie Grene, *Martin Heidegger* (London,
1957), p. 14.

notion now is through structuralist developments? In a word, Western philosophy needs the old and the tried, with the advances of the new.

The present discussion regarding the interpretation of existence has been set, accordingly, within a frame bounded by two of the modern extremes. On the one hand, existence has been presented to us in the bleak austerity of a logical auxiliary symbol. On the other, it has been projected with all the exhilarating richness of human freedom and subjectivity. Are not these both important facets that need every development philosophy can give them? Do they not fit into and enhance the role of existence as originally known through judgment? Does not the thinking of the past, expanded through the best in the present, enable one to attain here the most harmonious and satisfactory and far-reaching philosophical results?

Quickened in this throbbing matrix, why should not the meaning of existence continue to hold, philosophically, the spiritual destiny of the West? The standard English translation of Heidegger's question cited at the beginning of the present volume takes up again the phrase in the wording "the historical destiny of the West."[41] Heidegger may be hard enough to translate into German, and the further translation into English may be obliged to reflect considerable interpretation. In contrast to the inert character of matter, the notion of the spiritual in an existential setting may well require supplementary rendition as "historical." In fact, as the welfare state with its stress on material comfort moves on into the fulfillment society, may

---

[41] Heidegger, An Introduction to Metaphysics, tr. Ralph Manheim (New Haven: Yale University Press, 1959), p. 42 ("historical"). Cf. p. 37 ("spiritual"). In the German text, Einführung in die Metaphysik (Tübingen, 1953), pp. 28 and 32, the same word geistige is used in both places. In Heidegger the "Lichtungsgeschichte des Seins," as Hans Meyer, Martin Heidegger und Thomas von Aquin (Munich, etc., 1964), pp. 35–36, notes, gives the impression of too strong a conditioning by the present situation. In St. Thomas, on the contrary, the approach to existence is clearly free from restrictions caused by any bearing on a particular epoch, even though the temporal fluidity assures its historical character.

not the emphasis on individual destiny require a still stronger metaphysical underpinning and more profoundly fluid assessment of man in terms of the existential dimension? And as history pushes on further in a cosmopolitan spirit that transcends the limitations of merely Western tradition, may not the correct philosophical interpretation of existence be even more important for understanding the spiritual destiny of all mankind?

Index

151